YES YOU CAN...

JUST
CHANGE
IT!

PEGGY GRALL

Printed and bound by Transcontinental Inc. in Quebec, Canada.
Cover design by Rachel Colic www.rachelcolic.com & A Creative
Experience www.acreativeexperience.com

National Library of Canada Cataloguing in Publication

Grall, Peggy
        Just Change It! / Peggy Grall.

Includes bibliographical references.
ISBN 978-0-9734980-3-5

1. Self-actualization (Psychology) 2. Change (Psychology) I. Title.

BF637.C4G72 2004 158.1
C2004-902147-8

To learn more about Just Change It! programs and products please visit
www.JustChangeIt.com or call 1.866.949.6698

This book is dedicated to
Reba Juanita Grall (Aka my Mother)
Whose love and support have made
all the difference

Table of Contents

Go

Acknowledgements

THEY SAY IT takes a village to raise a child. Well, I can tell you that it takes a truck load of great friends, loving family and competent professionals to bring a book into the world. This book is truly the collaborative work of many hands.

My heart will forever be grateful to all the wonderfully courageous psychotherapy clients who have spent time with me working towards making personal changes in themselves and in their lives. Throughout my career I've been blessed by spending time with an array of clients who have shared their thoughts, feelings, challenges and triumphs with me, and I remain forever in their debt. Through their willingness to be open and trusting, I've been given the gift of observing the change process at its sublime best.

My coaching clients working in health care, retail, industry, non-profit, and the hallowed halls of academia have given me a rare glimpse behind the sometimes thin veil of this thing we call our work life. I've been privileged to listen, observe and talk with them in boardrooms, at conference centers, in private offices and on retreat. We've looked for solutions, made decisions and planned the next steps in large crowds and in small, intimate teams, huddled together. Thank you for allowing me to see your creative brilliance, your courage under fire and the passion that drives you and your organizations forward. By working with you I've been able to incorporate the best of professional change concepts into this book.

The professionals who have put their hands and hearts to this work have been more than generous with their time and talent. I want to thank Christine Tomaselli for her tenacious editing approach that made me think hard, Elizabeth Beveredge whose gentle nudges made me think twice, and Lisa Martynuik who is a whiz at managing details. I also want to thank Darlene Schacht for her talent and patience during the layout process.

We're blessed in this life if we're loved by our family …no matter what. In this respect, I know I'm truly blessed. My mother, to whom this book is dedicated, has taught me the meaning of unconditional support. Her belief in who I am has allowed me to hold my head high, even when I've run my own life into the ditch and struggled to start again…and again.

One's partner in life is often the person whose very presence demands that they make the most significant changes of all, and that's been true for me with my husband Graydon Estey. At times in the course of our relationship, I've been required to look more closely at myself than I've wanted to, but the changes that have been the hardest won, and the most liberating, have come through loving my husband. Thank you, Graydon, for supporting my efforts to produce this book—a manual of hope for other would—be changers.

As any parent will tell you, the most important lessons in life, are learned from our children. By watching mine grow I've seen again and again how people were meant to face life. From toddlers to teenagers, and now as adults, whom I not only love but respect, my children have given me the gift of their resilience. The personal life lessons that underpin this book were often learned at their expense. Thank you Dan, Loren and Rachel for being co-creators with me.

Tena Crow knows more about me and my ability to change—or not—than anyone on this earth. As I've moved through the changes in my own life she's the sister who has cried with me, laughed with me, been excited for me, worried about me and, at times, has been only too willing to confront and correct me. She has been completely *there* for me. She is a hairdresser by trade, but is the best darn therapist this gal has ever had.

My sanity and this book would not have been possible without the gentle support of my dear friend and mentor Mel Weldon. Whether he wanted to or not, Mel has served as a father figure to me for much of my adult life, and I'm better because of it. His extraordinary wisdom, accepting nature and undoubting spirit are always with me.

Many friends and colleagues have supported and advised me throughout this project. A special thanks to Kathleen Redmond, a good friend who has been a step ahead of me in the book writing process and who has been incredibly generous with her ideas, information, contacts and support.

Childhood girl friends are a woman's rare treasure, and I have been blessed with one of the best. Some of my most significant life changes have happened while in the company of Sue Jay. We met as little girls and to this day, no matter how many miles or years there are between us, we still *get* each other.

Everyone needs a friend they can laugh with. For me, that's Debbie Bartucci. Together we've weathered the challenges of divorce, teenagers, university (in that order) and now the daunting task of maturing gracefully. Many of my most difficult life lessons have been softened by sharing a hoot with Debbie.

If you know you've contributed to this book and my life, and I've forgotten to thank you—consider yourself thanked right now. Perhaps we met at a conference, sat next to each other at school, lived in the same neighborhood, attended the same church or shared a moment with each other at our children's daycare. If that was you—I thank you. If this book is helpful to a few or many, please know that you've had a hand in it.

Introduction

PEOPLE DREAM OF being different. They set goals and timelines in the hope of attaining their dreams, but sometimes mysteriously fail at what appears to be perfectly legitimate attempts at change. As a therapist, I've seen it over and over again.

Perhaps you've done the same thing—tried to change a behavior, situation or relationship, only to find yourself weeks or months later, alarmingly close to where you started. Why does this happen? Why is it so hard for people, even the most determined, to make *real* changes? Because making lasting personal or professional change *is hard*. Making real changes that stick, is the hardest work you'll ever do—but the good news is that **it is doable!**

Just Change It! is about real people like you making real changes. It's a book that will guide you, inspire you, make you laugh, and help you celebrate your change victories as you learn to overcome your negative behaviors, unproductive feelings, annoying habits or unsatisfactory relationships that just aren't working anymore.

Whether you've purchased this book out of curiosity or desperation, my hope is that there will be something in it that will help you manage the changes in your life more effectively.

This book is especially for you if you've tried to change something within yourself, or about your life in the past, and have been unsuccessful.

In my practice as a psychotherapist I've spent thousands of hours counseling and coaching people that have faced a myriad of sometimes exciting, and often difficult, life circumstances. I've worked with people who have overcome major issues like job loss, ill health, divorce, social prejudice, abuse and major financial set backs. And I've helped people manage particularly annoying issues such as dealing with an uncooperative co-worker, being passed over for a promotion, or being demoralized by damaging office gossip.

I've also worked with people who have wanted to change careers, start new relationships, get fit, learn a new skill or overcome their fear of success. In my work I've witnessed some very important and powerful ways people make changes to the way they think, feel and behave. I've been able to help people develop a solid change plan and acquire the support that they've needed to move their life forward. Looking back, I'm most proud of having helped people change those things about themselves and their lives that they never dreamed possible.

I've personally experienced dramatic changes and am keenly aware that changes come in all forms and intensities—some welcome, some not. Some lessons I've learned about change have been exhilarating, while others have been gut-wrenching. In my life I've survived unemployment, divorce, the sudden death of a parent, an earthquake and an attack at knifepoint.

I've also consciously *chosen* to change a lot of things. I left home at 18 and have moved about every two years since. I've changed jobs and even occupations several times. I continue to make major, annual overhauls to my personal style and rearrange the furniture in my home at the slightest whim.

I love the thrill of *the next thing*; I savor the sweetness of new beginnings. I look for opportunities to refine or discard old ideas and processes that no longer work. I'm constantly scanning the horizon for innovative approaches to improve the way I work, play, love and live. Maybe you've picked up this book because you're working towards, or would like to accomplish, some of these same things. Consider me as your personal change coach, helping you to successfully take each step towards your goal.

Within these pages, you'll find a number of great ideas on how to handle those changes that you didn't ask for, never thought would happen to you or haven't the foggiest notion how to manage. So whether you've been downsized, right sized or just plain fired, been left by a significant other—or done the leaving—received bad news about your health or lost a loved one, want to make a career change, get fit or overhaul your relationships, the ideas in this book have the power to help you achieve your goals…at last!

I believe in the power of human resiliency. I've been amazed and delighted to see how creative, buoyant and determined individuals can be when faced with a difficult set of circumstances or a truly audacious goal. I've witnessed great courage and stamina demonstrated by people who, when slammed with life's twists and turns or when choosing to reach for the stars, have crafted for themselves lives that are enriched and full—and you can too.

To maximize your experience using this book, I'm suggesting you take the next 21 days – about the time it takes to change a habit—and get into a change routine, like the one below.

- Find a quiet, comfortable place to read.

- Read one section a day.

- Reflect on the ideas in the section, and if you have purchased one of the *Fast Track* Workbooks that support the learning in this book, answer the questions in the corresponding sections as you read. If you are working directly from this book, at the end of each chapter ask yourself:

  How does this idea apply to me and my situation and what can I begin to do differently today as a result of what I have learned or realized?

- Then try one new thing each day.

Treat this book like a good friend—spend time with it —often. Carefully consider the advice it offers, allowing it to bring you joy and comfort and introduce it to others who might benefit from its content. I encourage you to contact me and let me know how **Just Change It** has helped you make a change in your life. I'm always fascinated to learn about the creative ways in which people craft their lives.

We can all succeed at change. In fact, when we put into place a solid plan, using the appropriate tools and seeking the right support, our success is virtually guaranteed!

There are convenient and useful workbooks on a variety of change topics to accompany **Just Change It**. The workbooks are designed to focus on a specific type of change such as:

Getting Fit
Navigating Separation and Divorce
Kicking Bad Habits
Career changes

The workbooks are designed to help by focusing you on your area of change through Exercises and Insight Building questions. If you'd like to purchase a workbook, log on to:

www.JustChangeIt.com

On
Your
Mark

Shift Happens

*"If you have no aspirations,
then your life will control you
rather than you controlling your life."*
~ *Author Unknown*

DID YOU KNOW that our bodies completely remake themselves every seven years? Every moment we're alive, we're in a constant renewal cycle. As we stand here on terra firma, our earth is circling around the sun, which hangs in a galaxy that is in motion within and beside other galaxies. Every living thing on the planet is exchanging molecules with every other living thing. An incredible choreography of motion surrounds us. For us to stand still, cling to and refuse to move and change, contradicts every natural law in the universe.

Whether we want *big, fat change*s in our lives or not – they happen! Whether you're choosing to change or being forced to change, the formula for success is largely the same.

People approach change in a variety of ways – especially the unsolicited kind. Some people want life to consist of years of uninterrupted sameness. So when they are faced with another wave of change, they withdraw, stall and become resentful – as if it shouldn't have happened.

Still others think that if they don't acknowledge it, and don't cooperate with it, the change will just go away. Putting your head in the sand only nets you a dirty face. Better to look around and face the new situation – with eyes wide open.

When a situation gets difficult, some people tell themselves that someone else needs to change, and that

3

they definitely don't need to. Hey, you can wait for others to 'see the light', 'smarten up' or 'come around', but you may be waiting for a very long time. And if this change that you're experiencing was initiated by someone else, then it's your move now.

At times, life in the *change lane* can feel like being strapped to a runaway roller coaster – both exciting and scary at the same time. Some days you'd just like to go home to mom and dad, slip into your old room, put on your favorite music and stare at the ceiling. So what's a fully-grown 'grown-up' supposed to do at times like these? I've got some ideas that you just might find helpful. Let's explore this territory together.

What's possible?

*"Far away there in the sunshine are my highest
aspirations. I may not reach them, but I can
look up and see their beauty, believe in them,
and try to follow where they lead."*
~ Louisa May Alcott

HOW BIG IS the change that you want to make? How
fabulous will it be when you've accomplished your goal?
Will you be shouting from the rooftops when this *thing*
you want to change, is changed? Will it rock your world to
achieve your goal, survive the event or overcome the losses
you've incurred? I hope so.

When I was a little girl I used to watch the Wonderful
World of Disney every Sunday night. Walt Disney's spirit of
optimism and his fabulous imagination influenced the world
as none had before him. He once said, "If you can dream it,
you can do it." Perhaps that's where Disney's famous, *When
You Wish Upon A Star,* theme song came from. I believed
then as I do now, that dreams indeed do come true. Do you?

My hope for you is that when this time of change in your life
is complete, you won't just be a *bit* better, but that you're going
to be completely and unbelievably awesome! My wish for you
is that you dream big and often, that you reach higher than you
think you can, and that you push farther than your friends think
you should or your family would have ever thought possible.

You bought this book for a reason. Perhaps you're telling
yourself that *this time* you're really going to make it. This
time you *will* succeed. That's a very good first step. I know
you can do it…. if you dream it. I want the change you make

5

this time to be a permanent one. As you work through this book, breathe in the rarified air of possibility, and stay open to your wildest dreams coming true.

Is it Time for a Change?

Has something or someone significant in your life changed?

Has your boss increased your workload or responsibilities? Is a co-worker beginning to irk you? Have your children left for university? Have you and your partner decided to separate? Has the bottom dropped out of property values in your neighborhood?

When people and circumstances around you change, it can be a great time to make a change for yourself. Often, when others or circumstances change, we simply *must* change in response.

Have your feelings of annoyance, frustration or anger at a particular situation, relationship or person intensified?

Are you discontent with your job, relationships or living arrangement, and now find yourself feeling angry and resentful? Or maybe those extra 15 pounds you've been carrying around are really beginning to bug you.

Anger, in any of its forms, is a red flag that means something or someone needs to change. That *someone* might just be you! You may be feeling angry because you've been allowing others to step over your personal boundaries too often, saying *yes* when you've wanted to say *no*, or taking on projects and responsibilities that really belong to others. Maybe you're angry because you've let yourself down before and taken the easy way out instead of really challenging yourself to become all you can.

Have trusted friends or family suggested that you need to make a change?

Perhaps a good friend has told you that you're behaving with your children in a hurtful or inappropriate manner. Or perhaps your partner has brought it to your attention that your drinking has increased lately and that your family is worried about you.

I don't recommend that people change for other people. Just because someone else thinks you need to change isn't reason enough to do it. However, if the people you love and trust in this world are telling you that there's something in your behavior or choices that are worrisome, I'd recommend that you *listen carefully.* Often, people close to us can see things that we can't; they can recognize opportunities that we might miss. When you get input from an outside source, consider it and then choose your actions wisely.

Is it just simply time to make a change, move on or step out?

Have you just graduated from school and are now ready to launch your career? Have you been in a healthy, long term relationship and now want to get married? Did you just turn 40 or 50? Are you looking for a better paying and more interesting job? Or are you starting to consider retirement?

Sometimes it's the season, age or stage of our lives that dictates the need for a change. For many people they make their best changes in response to life's milestones. What time is it in your life?

Has there been a major crisis or event that's propelling you towards change?

Have you received a negative health report, lost a loved one or been in an accident? Have you just won the lottery? Has your business failed, or taken a big leap forward necessitating some new strategies or purchases? Have your long time friends moved away, leaving you with the need to find some new ones?

Sometimes life's crises can propel us into some very important life reviews and changes. Often, when something big has happened, it's a great time to consider making other big changes. If you're on a roll—keep rolling!

Maybe you're just looking for something new, different, more challenging or fun!

7

Are you looking for an adventure to capture your attention? Would you like to sail around the world before you turn 40? Do you want to become CEO in the next year, climb Mt. Everest or learn to speak Spanish – just because you can?

Variety truly is the spice of life! If the change you want to make is just for the pleasure and excitement of it – go for it! If you're a natural change agent, you may make several significant changes in your life just to shake up the landscape. I've done that many times and can't wait for the next time!

Whatever your reasons, and they're all valid, only *you* can decide when you're ready to make a change.

Jack, a 46 year old accountant at a Fortune 500 company got some sobering health news from his doctor and decided that things had to change – and fast. The pace of his highly stressful job had left him with ulcers and high blood pressure. He was having trouble sleeping and couldn't seem to relax, no matter what he tried.

After a long talk with his wife, Jack decided to make a career move that he had dreamed about for years. He bought a small hobby farm outside the city and began to raise show dogs. He had always wanted to own a champion, so he purchased one and began going to shows and competing. He also decided to take advantage of a slower pace of life and the beautiful wide open spaces of his new surroundings to upgrade his fitness routine. He and his wife began running, slowly at first, but finally ramping up to eight miles a day. Within six months Jack was successfully entrenched in a new career that he loved, and had made huge strides to improve his fitness routine. What had started out as bad news from his doctor had become a complete lifestyle make-over.

Is it time for a change in your life? If not, do yourself a favor and simply put the book away and save it for when you are *really* ready. Don't play at making a change, that only leads to frustration and embarrassment and may burn out the change buddies that you'll need when you're more serious. It's OK if you're not ready yet.

7 Naked Truths About Change

"Nothing changes, if nothing changes."
~ Melody Beatte

BOLT YOURSELF IN because I'm about to tell you what your mother never did about life, people and making change. That's right, the naked truth. It's important that you know about these realities *before* you dip your toes in the pool of transformation.

Naked Truth #1
Your approach to change may need upgrading.

"When you're through changing, you're through."
~ Bruce Barton

Do you usually embrace change, resist it, or take a neutral 'wait and see attitude'? Where do you fit in the following descriptions?

About 30% of the population will resist change, regardless of what the change is. They see it coming and run as far and as fast as they can, or they dig in and stubbornly oppose all efforts to move them. These people just don't like change.

When faced with change, 50% of the population takes a neutral position. They don't run after new ideas and ways of doing things, but don't actively resist them either. These people are characterized by:

- a *wait and see attitude* to most situations,

9

- a need for all the facts to be in hand before making a move,
- a general sense of reserved curiosity and half-hearted support for anything and anyone new.

The remaining 20% of the population is 'change friendly'. These are the people who welcome change and push themselves, and the needed changes forward. These are the natural **change agents**. They're people who are:

- flexible, realistic, good communicators,
- eager for improvement, excited by new ideas,
- steady at riding out difficult transitional feelings and conditions,
- quick to make the most of opportunities,
- excited by personal challenges.

Whichever group you're in—there's good news. You can switch groups any time you want! You can challenge your old ideas and responses to change and adopt more flexible ones.

If your old approach to change is outdated or limiting and is holding you back—give it up! A healthier attitude is just a decision away.

Naked Truth #2
Initiating change is preferable to having it forced on you.

*"Faced with the choice
between changing one's mind
and proving that there is no need to do so,
almost everybody gets busy on the proof."*
~ *John K. Galbraith*

When you sense that the winds of change are blowing in your life – get ready! Don't hide from it, deny that it's happening or pretend you don't see it. It's a lot better to initiate change while you can, than to try to react and adjust to it later. The sooner you let go of the status quo, the easier the transition will be.

Before I learned to relish change and I would see an unwanted change coming, I'd tell myself, "This will blow over. I don't need to do anything. I'll just wait it out." Guess what —the change happened anyway. What's worse is that my *wait-and-see* attitude often resulted in my missing opportunities to create parts of the change the way I would have wanted them.

Those who learn to anticipate and embrace change and quickly adapt to it will thrive; those who resist it will perish. If you're mindful in your life and conscious about what's happening around you, you won't be taken by surprise so often.

I believe that a good number of people are psychologically asleep. They go through their days saying and doing what they've always said and done; they think, believe and react in the same ways that their parents did. They rarely examine their own behavior or question their own motives, and they don't look for alternative ways of handling challenging situations. When they hit a rough spot, they just do more of what they've always done. When asked why they've made the choices they've made, or done what they've done, they'll often say, "that's just who I am." End of discussion. They're asleep. They fell into their coma

11

early in life and unless a bomb goes off in their lives to act as a wake-up call, they'll go to their graves asleep.

Many insight-less people inhabit this earth. Don't be one of them. The problem with being insight-less is that you end up creating much of your own misery. Every time you make an unconscious decision or shelter yourself from seeing the truth, you will end up in a big mess. Be nicer to yourself than that.

Naked Truth #3
People don't change for other people.

"I love you, you're perfect—now change."

Contrary to your favorite soap opera or romance novel, *people don't change for other people*. Sorry to 'burst your bubble', but the research bears it out. Most people have a hard enough time changing for themselves, let alone someone else.

A young client wanted to learn how to be more sociable. Terrific goal. Later it surfaced that it was her fiancé who wanted her to make these changes – preferably before the wedding. He wanted her to be funnier and more entertaining. He wanted her to be the life of the party. She was shy, intelligent, focused and intense. The 'new' her would have been 180° different than who she really was. She tried it for a while and then came to realize that she felt phony and out of step with herself.

Are you tempted to become what someone else wants you to become? Most try it at least once in a life – and realize it's a big mistake!

Naked Truth #4

Change yourself

> *"Let him that would move the world,*
> *first move himself."*
> ~ *Socrates*

You can't change anyone but yourself. People may say they'll change because you want them to, they may even try. Ultimately successful change comes from a deep acceptance of, and commitment to, one's self.

Consider this ageless wisdom:

When I was a young man, I wanted to change the world.
I found it was difficult to change the world—so I tried to change my nation.
When I found I couldn't change my nation—I began to focus on my town.
I couldn't change the town...
And so, as an older man, I tried to change my family.
Now, as an old man, I realize the only thing I can change is myself.
And now I realize that, if long ago I had changed myself
I could have had an impact on my family
My family and I could have made an impact on our town.
That impact could have changed our nation and ...
I could have changed the world.
- Unknown

It's estimated that about 30% of the people in your world can directly influence how you behave and the decisions you make. So it stands to reason then, that you can influence others as well. The operative word here is *influence* – not change. You can influence those closest to you to make changes, sometimes in a fairly dramatic way. Sometimes seeing you change will inspire movement by others. If others make changes because of what you do—bonus! But, start with yourself first.

13

Naked Truth #5
Feelings can sometimes be misleading.

"If you're going through hell, keep going."
~ *Sir Winston Churchill*

One of the key reasons that people fail at their efforts to make lasting change is that they simply aren't willing to stick it out, do the hard work, put in the hours and keep moving towards their goal—regardless of how they *feel* at the moment.

There was a time when I thought things had to *feel right* for them to *be right*. I thought that unless I felt excited, motivated and *ready* or *on track* with the next step in a particular change plan, that I shouldn't proceed. You want the truth? Often the next step in your change program won't *feel right*…even when it *is right*. In fact sometimes it may be painful, boring or costly to take that next step.

Jeremy was a bright young sales associate at a pharmaceutical company when he was sent to me for coaching. He had just completed a 360° Assessment process and the feedback from his superiors was less than stellar. Jeremy's VP said that his enthusiasm and willingness to tackle large accounts was being hampered by his lack of organizational skills. Jeremy had been hoping to secure the national sales director position that was opening up in a few months. Instead of taking the 360° feedback seriously, he minimized it, remarking that his ability to charm clients far outweighed his need to 'get every little detail right'.

Although a lack of organizational skills had always been a problem for him, Jeremy thought that the company should take their chances and promote him anyway. The company's national accounts represented a significant percentage of their annual revenue and management wasn't willing to take a risk that Jeremy would loose a key client. Human Resources offered him a development plan in which he would be mentored and coached for a period of 9 months, with a review at the end of that time to evaluate his readiness for promotion.

14

In our initial meeting Jeremy was sullen and dismissive. He began the session by recounting his sales numbers for the last quarter and telling me how 'this whole thing just didn't feel right' and that he 'just knew' he was ready to take on larger accounts. Unfortunately Jeremy chose to go with his feelings and he left the company to look for greener pastures. I saw him at a conference about a year later and he told me that when he left, he had accepted a senior level sales position in another company and within a few months had been sent back to inside sales due to, you guessed it, his lack of organizational skills.

If the next step in your change plan is hard, repetitive or boring and you're tempted to by-pass it…Stop! Do you need to do this before you can tackle what's next? If so, hang in there, get serious and do it—no matter how it feels right now.

Naked Truth #6
You must travel in the Change Lane
on the way to your goal.

"One does not discover new lands without consenting to lose sight of the shore for a very long time."
~ Marilyn Ferguson, American futurist

Beyond the safety of the *known*, out past the headlights of the status quo, there's a stretch of life's highway that everyone must travel on the way to their goals.

Remember the story of The Ten Commandments? The Israelites had been in slavery for hundreds of years, pleading to God to deliver them from their life of hardship. Finally, when God told Moses to lead his people out of their misery, they left Egypt in joyous celebration of the possibilities they would encounter in the 'Promised Land'.

As the story goes, the Israelites wandered through the wilderness for a full 40 years before crossing into the new land.

At many points along the way, they complained to Moses for leading them away from their home and out into the wilderness. After a while, they even began to beg Moses to take them back to their slave masters. It wasn't until the entire generation that had originally left Egypt had died, that they were able to muster the courage to actually go and live in the land that had been promised to them. They had begged for decades to be released from slavery to the Egyptians, and when they were finally on their way, they got scared!

Welcome to the change process! This is very much what it feels like to make a significant personal change. If you travel very far in the direction you want to go, at times you may want to go back!

The *change lane* is that strip of life's highway that you occupy when you shift into high gear and move past those with whom you've been traveling. It's a time when you assert your intention to move into a different place—a different way of acting and feeling to ultimately end up on a new stretch of highway. Life moves fast here. It's unpredictable and uncertain, but it's also very cool! You can feel the power of your passion and dreams here; you call upon parts of yourself that are often kept in reserve, waiting for the right time to *Go*!

The *change lane* is characterized by:

- anxiety and lapses in motivation,
- disorientation and self-doubt,
- the re-emergence of old, unresolved issues, and
- personal and professional vulnerability.

The change lane is that place where you aren't yet solid in a new way of thinking, a new behavior or set of circumstances, and yet you know you can never return to the way it used to be.

There's no real way to avoid it, and there's only one way to get through this part, and that's by going *through* it.

During intense change people can find themselves floundering in the deep waters of human transformation, becoming frustrated, scared and distracted. Sometimes people begin to question their original intentions, lose contact with their support systems and succumb to the temptation of settling for *half-way*. It's in this emotional territory where the real change happens, or not.

This uncomfortable, scary, uncharted territory is exactly where you must be prepared to spend some time in order to get where you want to go. It's a place filled with unanswered questions and unclear boundaries; it's an experiment of untested theories with unknown outcomes. This part of the journey requires faith in yourself, and when you can't muster that—you must have faith in your plan. It's in this place— this new, unreal, uncertain, unpredictable place—where real change happens. The most profound shifts occur when you're stripped of the familiar, positionally vulnerable and emotionally naked.

Change can be scary. The changes you're making might just make people uncomfortable, and for sure they'll make you uncomfortable, for a while anyway! People often describe this uncomfortable, in-between time in the change process by saying things like, "I'm not the way I used to be, but I'm not *yet* how I want to be," or "I don't know who I am anymore," or "I feel so unsettled, anxious and unsure of myself." Nothing is predictable in this place!

The good news is that this is also the place where creativity is at its peak. Necessity really is the mother of invention. When you're out there on the edge, you're primed to formulate new ideas, risk new responses and harness your anxiety to make it work for you. When you get to this unfamiliar place—hang on dear traveler, you're making progress!

Naked Truth #7
Be yourself

"Ride the horse in the direction that it's going."
~ *Werner Erhard*

Changing should mean becoming more of who you really are. Whether you're choosing to lose weight, change jobs or careers, move to a new house or continent, get in or out of a relationship, volunteer with a new group or buy or sell something, you should ask yourself this critical question: "Will this bring me closer to my best self?" If the answer is *yes*—move forward. If the answer is *no*, then reconsider your actions. Are you trying to become someone else? Change programs and initiatives should be efforts to uncover, discover and reveal more of who you truly are, otherwise they are destined to fail.

Kevin was a bright young engineer in a large manufacturing company who wanted to upgrade his leadership skills so he could achieve the management position on his design team. He saw the opportunities for advancement in his company and thought more money and status would be just the right move for him. His career was progressing nicely and he was highly valued for his technical expertise.

When Kevin came to me for coaching we looked closely at his personality profile and I asked him about his values and what he felt was important in his life. He talked passionately about his wife, the small house in the country that they had bought and their desire to begin a family. Being a father had been a goal of his for many years, but Kevin also wanted very much to be a manager.

Kevin worked hard and secured the new position in his company. However, he soon realized that the long hours required to perform his new job were beginning to take him away from his wife and the activities that they both enjoyed. He began to have trouble sleeping and found himself extremely stressed. I asked him to look again at why he had

18

chosen advancement as a goal and how he saw himself fitting into that new lifestyle. After some serious review, he realized that although he could clearly do the job, the lifestyle that went with it wasn't compatible with his true nature. The long hours were taking him farther away from his more central goals of having a satisfying family life.

We are incredible beings with the capacity to accomplish just about anything we try. But remember, a worthy change effort is one that enhances your natural gifts and aligns with your deepest held values.

Now you know the Naked Truth about making change. I hope it didn't hurt too much. Better to know it now, than get caught with your transformational pants down! So, what will you do with what you know? Information without insight—is philosophy! What do these truths mean to you? What do you need to do differently today?

Trust the Process

"The difference between 'involvement' and 'commitment' is like an eggs-and-ham breakfast: the chicken was 'involved'—the pig was 'committed'."
~ Unknown

SUCCESS HAD ALWAYS *come easily to Cameron. He was captain of the debate team, excelled at sports in high school, and finished in the top three in his class in university. He was also the first to land the 'dream job' soon after graduation and it wasn't long before the company was offering him a promotion and a new title. He was the Generation X poster boy. He was on his way to the top...fast. While returning from a business trip to the coast, he opened his e-mail in flight to find a message marked 'urgent'. The message simply read, "The board has decided to take the company in a different direction and your services will no longer be required after today. Please report to Human Resources upon your arrival for processing out."*

He sat stunned for the remainder of the flight. He hadn't anticipated this. No matter how he turned it around in his head, he just couldn't make sense of it. The company was doing well; he was doing well. Over the next few weeks, Cameron experienced what most people do when they're hit with the sudden and surprising decisions of others.

If you're reading this book because someone has made decisions that have directly and dramatically affected you, then this section will be very important for you to understand. When presented with unexpected events, people move through several predictable stages on their way to adjustment. Each stage represents a normal step in the process of moving from where

21

you are, to where you really want to be, and people will take differing amounts of time to move from one stage to the next.

How Change Happens

In this chapter and the next I'm giving you two different ways to look at the process of change: The Cycle of Change and, the Grief and Loss Cycle of Change. Both are explanations of how people move through the process of transforming themselves, each with its own emphasis.

The first model, The Cycle of Change represents my observations of how people begin, continue and finally complete a personal or professional change program of their own choosing. The second model, The Grief and Loss Cycle of Change is an examination of how people process the emotions of an unwanted change or a particularly difficult change program.

Successful change happens in a somewhat predictable sequence. In the following model, you'll notice that the ovals overlap and intersect, demonstrating the fluid nature of each step in the change process, one step leading to another. Each stage is distinct, and yet links to the next as if to invite it. Often, people move through a stage and then find that they've looped back for a brief period of time to a previous stage before permanently moving on to the next.

Inertia

Ever notice how teenagers can lie on a couch all day, never moving a muscle, regardless of the life going on around them? That's my image of inertia—a state of immobility, and a time when the status quo is king. This quiet before the storm occurs just before the *Big, Fat Change*—before the announcement is made, the letter comes, the police call, the meeting happens, the words are said, the diagnosis is confirmed, the fight happens, or before you *find out*. This is the time just before we have to face the fact that things have changed.

Before we choose to change, there's a time when we're at rest—perhaps content, or unaware that a change is coming, or that we need to make a change. For some, this time lasts for years. For others, even before the remnants of the last change are fading away, they're already fashioning the next. Some say ignorance is bliss and that what you don't know can't hurt you. I think it's smart to keep your eyes trained on the horizon of your life, looking for the next wave and the next time you'll need to, or want to, make a change.

Cycle of Change

INERTIA
"I don't get it"
Unaware of the need
to change

INFORMATION
"I see"
"Ah-Ha" moments
Conscious of Old
behaviors

INTEGRATION
"I'm doing it"
Practice and Mastery
Of New behavior

INITIATION
"I'll try it"
Face the Fear
Risk
Take Action

INSIGHT
"I get it"
New Decision
Count the Cost
Make a Plan

Information

Gathering information is a critical part of any successful change effort. The information phase of a change is the time when you seek new ideas, knowledge or input. Information may come to you via a friend, a colleague, a thought-provoking movie, article or song. For you to *do* things differently, you must *see* things differently, and that's going to require that you take in some new information. Perhaps the information will come unsolicited—a friend tells you

23

that your partner is having an affair, your doctor warns you about your weight, your financial planner wants to explain the shortfall in your retirement plan, or your manager notifies you about a promotion opportunity. Solicited or not, this is the kind of information that nudges, or blasts you into the next phase. New information invites new insights, which pave the way for powerful change.

Insight

Many of us have stood by and watched the people we care about get some critical information about a situation that needs to change, only to watch them sweep it *under the carpet* and never apply it to themselves.

Insight is that ability to know how the new information applies to you. It's the moment in time when you *get it*, when you *know* what you haven't known before. It's the moment in time when you see for the first time what's really happening and what needs to be done. It's a time when your perspective on your job, financial situation, skill set, social life, relationship with kids, friends, God or yourself is illuminated. Some part of your life has shifted. You know now what you didn't before. Maybe it's because you sought out the information so that you could know; or someone, or some event, dumped the truth in your lap.

This is a time of clarity—a time when it feels like the fog has lifted and the world is sharper and more in focus. However you come by the new information, knowledge, wisdom or perspective, the end result is the same—you must respond.

Initiation

True insight necessitates a response. When people *know* differently, they *do* differently. If your insights have shed new light on your life, work, health, relationships or spiritual situation and you don't like what you see—then it's time to *do something differently*. This part of the change process is where the pondering stops and the planning begins. This is when you count the costs, make key decisions, set goals and timelines, choose support systems and gather your change tools. This is the action part of the journey.

Integration

Changing *for real,* means to keep on—keeping on. The integration part of the journey is the time when your new thoughts, behaviors and routines become second nature. No longer a novice, you're now a savvy changer. You consistently do what works and you gain strength and expertise as you move forward. You know where the dark alleys and the danger zones are and you consistently take care of yourself, have fun and keep yourself ready for the twists and turns that all change efforts bring. The final 'hurrah' is realized when the *new* becomes *normal.*

The Grief and Loss Cycle of Change

"In any contest between power and patience,
bet on patience."
~ *W.B. Prescott*

WITH ALL MAJOR change comes loss, and with loss comes the need to grieve. That's right. Even though you may have wanted this change, when it comes to actually making a change, or responding to the unsolicited changes of others, loss is part of the process.

The grief/change process is like floating down a river. Sometimes you're in fast, churning water, feeling tossed and thrown around emotionally. However, as you continue through the process, you can find yourself in amazingly calm, deep water – a time for reflection. Then suddenly, you may be picked up and carried off again into the swift currents of hard work, social strain and personal pressure. This is especially true for people navigating unsolicited change.

In the 1960s, Elizabeth Kubler-Ross in her landmark book, *On Death and Dying,* outlined a model of grieving that demonstrated how people handle a major loss or a major change in their lives. She found there were predictable behavioral patterns that emerged. Since her initial work, there's been a tremendous amount of discussion about the nature of grief/change/loss, and the linear nature of the Kubler-Ross model has been challenged. Humans are very complex when they're transforming. This doesn't eliminate the need to have a solid plan with sequential steps, it just means that you must allow for the *real life* twists and turns of the journey.

Using the descriptions below, identify your feelings regarding the changes in your life. Which step best describes you *right now*? Do you recognize the feelings and behaviors associated with that phase of the transition? Read the descriptions that follow and look for ideas on how to move through each stage more easily and quickly.

Stability

   Shock/ Denial

      Anger/Bargaining/Depression

         Exploration

           Acceptance

Stability

This refers to the time before the change event happened—before the letter came, the phone rang, she said what she said, they left, he died, the announcement was made, the report was read, or you announced your decision. It's characterized by steadiness, routine, predictability and the *status quo*. In today's world this stage has become increasingly brief. Often people are in continuous, overlapping cycles of intense, change-producing events.

Shock and Denial

People go into varying degrees of shock and denial when a sudden change has begun. This stage in the change process is characterized by disbelief, confusion, fear, immobility and limited communication. Also during this stage, an individual or group may try to minimize the need to change or the complexity of the change. You may find yourself saying things like, "This won't last. They can't do this," or "They'll change their minds soon."

Denial is a refusal to face reality—a temporary defense against the confusion and shock caused by a major loss or major change. During this stage, people will often physically or psychologically isolate themselves. They'll pull into themselves, almost as if they're trying to absorb the shock of the situation.

Help yourself by taking time to get used to this change. Breathe, take long, hot baths, and walk. Remind yourself of other times when you've weathered difficulty. Don't make big decisions right now. Lean on your friends—their view of the situation will be clearer than yours right now.

Check yourself for signs that you're acting as if this situation hasn't happened. Welcome the advice of good friends who can provide you with *reality checks*.

Anger

Although I've said that the process of change is not sequential, with one step neatly following another, often a period of intense anger and frustration follows shock and denial. Anger is a natural emotion that often surfaces when the change is unwelcome. People can be angry at family, a company, co-workers, leaders or themselves. Subtle forms of expressing anger can include missing appointments and deadlines, *forgetting* important information, sabotaging change efforts, gossiping at the office or with friends, or withholding support from co-workers, friends or family. More obvious forms of anger include seeking revenge, being verbally or physically abusive or blaming others.

Feelings of anger, rage, envy and resentment are often directed at the person driving the change, or sometimes even God. The question most often asked in this stage is, "Why me?" People often twist reality and look for scapegoats in this part of the journey. Efforts by family and friends to reach out to those caught in this phase are often rebuffed or ignored.

Bargaining

This stage is marked by efforts to hold off the changes by offering informal trade-offs or making deals that will nullify the need for the change. It represents an attempt to keep the change from happening or being real.

For many people, when the emotions have lessened in intensity, they begin a process of trying to return to the way things used to be, or crafting another view of the future that's more acceptable. Simply put—they begin to bargain.

I was counseling a middle aged female client who wanted to return to school. Her children were in high school, and she wanted to begin a second career. Her husband spent a great deal of time trying to bargain his way out of this change. He didn't want the change to happen, and he began a campaign to modify his wife's plans. He suggested part-time school or putting off her return to university until the kids left home. He was essentially bargaining with his wife, since her changes were going to change his life! I've seen people bargain with partners, bosses, children, and police – anyone they think can stop the change.

When bargaining fails to yield the sought after results, most people give up. Letting go of bargaining attempts is both the good news and bad news for many people. Giving up the struggle against the change can create a sense of powerlessness. If they have really invested themselves in halting the change effort, people can feel that they are *giving in* and therefore *giving up* on themselves. This can create a general sense of sadness and apathy for a while.

Depression

When people can see that an unwanted change is really going to happen, they can feel helpless in the face of it. There are losses associated with any change, and loss creates the need to grieve and let go. One's energy is more internally focused at this point.

To move through this phase, feel what you feel, whatever that is. Cry when you need to cry, scream when you can be alone to do it, and pound pillows instead of faces! Feel it all in a safe and supportive environment. Make a tentative plan for beginning to handle the situation, then have someone you trust review your plan and give you feedback. Ask others how they've successfully handled a similar situation.

This is a difficult time for many people. Check yourself for significant changes in weight gain/loss, mood, sleep habits, the ability to focus and make decisions, energy level and desire to socialize. If you discover that you're experiencing a definite shift in these areas of your daily functioning, you'll want to consult a health care professional. Help yourself by letting others help you.

Exploration

When people have reached the end of bargaining—when they get sick and tired of being sick and tired—they'll begin to explore their options. They ask questions, seek out information and develop a genuine interest in how they can fit into the new way of doing things. They begin to talk to others about how they're handling the change, looking for clues as to how to move along the path.

This stage is characterized by people inquiring how the change will affect them and how they can assimilate the new process, goals or requirements of the change. People begin to look to the future and experiment with ways to fit themselves into the change plans. Energy begins to be externally focused at this point.

They accept that the change is happening, and that it's *they* who must change or be left behind. They start to make small, calculated moves toward the new way. They enter the mainstream again and begin to realize the benefits of the change, sometimes appreciating for the first time that life just might be better this new way.

At this point you start to come to terms with this *big, fat change*. This part of the journey feels good! Now is the time when you can play with your options. You can explore new opportunities that are available to you. Perhaps there are classes to take, groups to join, skills to upgrade, or new people to meet.

Acceptance

This is the final stage of the transition process and it's marked by optimism, energy and a willingness to risk new behaviors. During this time, people seek to learn the new skills necessary for them to be successful, as well as generating new ideas to add to the change effort.

If you've made it to this stage, give yourself a big pat on your hard working back! Relax, look around—you made it! You may even be up for helping others to assimilate a change in their lives. Yes, there's more work to be done, but the hard part is over. Now you can begin to move rapidly in a new direction.

Dream Big and Often

*Once upon a time there was a frog who lived in a big
ocean, who traveled to see a frog who lived in a ditch.
Soon after the Ocean Frog had arrived, the Ditch Frog
said boasting "Watch this."*
*With one leap, the Ditch Frog jumped down into
a puddle of water, swam across to the other side, and
jumped back onto the bank.*
*He proudly looked at the Ocean Frog and said,
"What do you think of that?"*
The Ocean Frog said, "Very impressive."
*The Ditch Frog said, "What's it like
where you live?"*
*The Ocean Frog said, "I'll have to
take you there."*

IF YOU'VE LIVED a portion or most of your life in a *ditch,*
it's sometimes hard to believe that the *ocean* really exists. If
you've been a victim in an abusive family, had a dead-end
job, lived in a dangerous neighborhood and felt fearful of
every move; you may not believe that you can have a life of
freedom, joy, success and personal power. Well, you can.

Here's a good first step to help you begin to see
yourself achieving your goal. It's called the Miracle Question
technique. The Miracle Question is an effective way of
inviting yourself into the change you want to make. Here's
the question:

*What would you do if suddenly one of your toughest
problems no longer existed, and/or your goal was finally
achieved? Imagine waking up tomorrow morning with
absolutely no trace of the problem, and/or being surrounded*

by the obvious evidence that your goal has been achieved. Describe your feelings and actions.

By *trying on* life with your goal achieved, or without *the problem,* you can smell, taste, feel and breathe in a different head space.

This is a very powerful exercise that has made a notable impact on many of my clients. When given the opportunity to try on a new frame of mind, I've seen snarky teens vividly describe how they would be responsible, loving and respectful if *the problem* were gone. I've witnessed emotionally distant spouses openly weep as they feel the emotions that they have kept at bay, once *the problem* wasn't there any more.

The real miracle is that, somewhere inside, you know exactly how you would *be* if you weren't how you *are* right now! You have the inner visionary power to create that place in your head and in your life.

So, close your eyes and get rid of *the problem.* Bring your goal into focus. Boom! You're free! It's done. You're there! Now descrbe it...

- What does it feel like?
- How are you different?
- Who/what is with you that wasn't before?
- Who/what has left?
- What do you say and do that's new, exciting and inspiring that you didn't used to do?
- Which of these new activities would actually reinforce the change?
- What are others saying?
- How do you feel about yourself? Others?
- What opportunities are presenting themselves?
- Who would notice? Who wouldn't?

Paint a vivid mental picture of how life would be if this *thing* that has been begging for a change were fixed, gone, solved, accomplished or completed. Journal in detail how you would feel, act, make decisions or treat other people. Which daily activities would no longer be necessary, what new things would you begin doing instead?

Allow yourself to soak in this new place—your rightful territory. Get familiar with how it feels, how you act and how powerful you are here. While you're working through this book, spend at least 15 minutes a day visualizing the end result—and watch the miracle unfold!

Passionate Pursuits

"We specialize in the wholly impossible."
~ Nannie Helen Burroughs

FOR MANY PEOPLE goal setting is a playful afterthought to New Years Eve. As the old year draws to a close they quickly think of something in their life they wish were different and vow to change it. They talk about it for a few weeks, maybe even make a few phone calls or attend a few classes and by mid February are comfortably back into their old routines. If this sounds like you—you're not alone.

Knowing where you're going is half the battle to getting there. So what do you want to change? Maybe someone else has done some changing lately and it now means that you have to make some decisions for yourself. Choose a passionate pursuit, one that gets your heart racing. If you don't feel some stirring in your soul to make this thing happen now, then the rough hills of reality may just do you in. If there isn't any passion, fire or excitement about this endeavour, then my advice is to give it up. Choose something else.

I encourage people to work on only one goal at a time. You might be able to change several things at once, but systematically working on one at a time allows you to focus all of your energy and ensures your success.

Here are the fundamentals of good goal setting:

A. Make sure it's *your* goal.

B. Write your goal down on paper; be specific and use positives terms. *Don't do it* goals don't work for most people.

C. Choose an objective that's large enough to
be inspiring and small enough to be doable.

D. Evaluate the goal on the following criteria:

    a) Is it specific—so that you can
actually experience, touch and feel your goal?

    b) Is it measurable – so that you'll know if you've
been successful?

    c) Is it challenging, yet realistic?

    d) Is it doable within a certain timeline?

Keep your goals *front-and-center*, write them on posters, stickies or 3x5 cards – whatever method will bring them in front of you on a regular basis (we are creatures with short memories). Have fun!

Over the years I've developed a fun and energizing way to set goals and it has become one of the most enjoyable things I do for myself. Between Christmas and New Years, every year, I set aside a full day to set goals for the year ahead. I take the phone off the hook, put on my favorite music, lock the doors and play! I surround myself with old magazines, articles, pictures of events and family, keepsakes and a large piece of poster board. I start by looking over last year's goals. I look for successes and short falls. I debrief the effort I put into them and try to uncover why I was successful at reaching some goals and not others.

I then begin to thumb through the magazines, relishing the pictures, remembering the events and reading snippets from inspirational literature. Then when I feel ready (you just know when you are) I cut out anything that seems to jump out at me – setting all of those pieces aside in a pile. Next, I paste my clippings on the poster board wherever they seem to fit. If there doesn't seem to be a good place for a particular piece, I toss it. Then I add words, phrases, free-hand drawing—which is a stretch because I'm no artist—until the poster looks complete.

This left brain activity never ceases to amaze me. Often I will have cut something out that didn't appear to have any significance in the cutting, only to discover its meaning when placed on the board. For instance, a picture of a radiant

50 year-old woman may come to represent wisdom and self confidence to me. A piece of costume jewellery might symbolize playfulness or a renewed commitment to financial freedom. A discarded Lego piece brings to mind my desire to spend time with my children and grandchildren.

When the poster is complete, I take a walk, have lunch and stretch. Then I turn my attention to the business of capturing my goals on paper. I choose only four for the entire year – that's always been plenty for me. When I'm done I step back and take a look from across the room. I ask myself these questions:

- Am I attracted to these goals?
- Do they excite me?
- Is this the best I can do?

If I can give a resounding 'yes' to all three questions—the poster goes up on my wall where it stays all year. I look at the picture version of my goals daily and review the written version quarterly. No magic to the method; but it's fun and it works for me.

Next, I suggest that you create an *operational description* of your goals. All you'll need for this exercise is a piece of paper, a pencil and your imagination. Use the following questions to discover and ellaborate on your goal.

1. Describe each goal in detail.
2. Specifically, what needs to be different?
3. What will you feel like when you've accomplished these?
4. Exactly what will you be doing differently?
5. How will others be reacting to you differently?
6. How will you feel about yourself when you've accomplished your goals?
7. What opportunities will open up to you as a result of achieving your goals?

Describing how your life will be when you've completed each goal gives you a glimpse into your future—and that's exciting!

Expect the Best

"Happiness is but a state of mind, and any time
you want you can cross the state line."
~ Waitin For You, Bob Dylan

CHANGE IS LIKE football. Often the best defense is a good offense. That is, when you're in a particularly difficult spot, expecting the best often invites the best to happen. Have you ever found yourself saying, "I knew this would happen," when something unwanted came your way? Don't invite trouble; invite success instead.

I am going to suggest that you adopt a Pollyanna attitude. That's right! For those of you familiar with the original story of Pollyanna, written by Eleanor Hodgman, you know that Pollyanna was a little girl who lost her parents early in life and was raised by a harsh and dutiful maiden aunt. Despite her misfortunes, Pollyanna brought sunshine to all the adults in her life because she refused to see their limitations, disabilities, or the obstacles in their lives. Her optimism was infectious. The sad, the lonely, the sick, and the obnoxious all became enamored with this little girl's enthusiasm and zeal.

Think back to a time when you were facing a difficult situation in which you just knew everything would turn out well, even though at the time, there was no tangible evidence to suggest that it would. Been there? Now ask yourself:

Were you better off anticipating a good outcome?

Did being optimistic hurt you in any way?

Did holding a positive attitude keep you from:

41

a) making good choices,

b) risking when you needed to, or

c) weathering the tough emotions involved?

Adults sometimes pooh-pooh this child-like perspective in favor of what they think is a more 'mature' or 'realistic' approach. Is it really more *mature* to focus on the negative in a situation? Is it more *realistic* to expect bad things to happen, and actually spend time looking for them? Does that really make sense? I think there is immense value in choosing optimism over pessimism? And really—don't we always have that choice?

Focus on Today

*"To live in the present is to live as if
the past never existed
and as if the future were irrelevant."*
~ *John Kuypers*

MANAGING A PERSONAL transition calls for extreme living. Extreme living means learning to live in the moment – right here and right now! Don't borrow trouble from the past or the future. Easy to say – tough to do.

Inevitably our life unfolds according to our focus. When you keep your eyes trained on past events, old problems and former disappointments, it's impossible to clearly see the path ahead. Conversely, continuing to strain your vision into the next few years and beyond, always trying to predict what will or might happen, or worse yet, what you hope *won't* happen, robs you of the power and beauty of *now*.

Your ability to effectively manage the change you're in is directly related to your ability to focus on the issues at hand. Right *here* and right *now* there are decisions to be made, things to be done, people to be reckoned with, plans to create, feelings to be felt and experiences to be lived. Staying present ensures that your full capacity of skills, intuition and insight are available to you. Change agents know that grabbing hold of the immediate—while maintaining an informed view of what may lay ahead—is the recipe for success.

Courage and Other Unnatural Acts

"The way out—is through."
~ Carl Jung

I'VE GOT SOME bad news and some good news about transforming yourself. The bad news is that you will feel fear on this journey. The good news? Fear is normal—and it won't kill you! During a change, everyone feels it – and everyone wishes they didn't. If you grow in any area of your life, you're guaranteed to feel fear along the way.

I've found that there are common themes to the fear people feel when they're making a change or transitioning through the changes created by others. What are you afraid of? Perhaps it's one or more of the following:

- appearing foolish
- losing *stuff,* friends, respect
- shaky finances
- pain: emotional, physical
- what else might happen
- success or failure

Facing fear actually diminishes fear. The difference between those who get frozen in their fear and those who don't, is that those who conquer fear do so by stepping into it. Stepping up to intense emotions can, at times, seem counter intuitive. At times you may feel like the best thing you can do is to bury your feelings and avoid anything that may make you more fearful. I invite you to do just the opposite. It's been my experience that if you run from the fearful things in your life, you will always be running from something. If, on the other hand, you stand up to your feelings of fear—and resolve to *do it anyway*—you'll break the grip that fear has on you. It doesn't get easier the longer you wait, and facing your fear sooner is better than later.

FEAR is
False
Evidence
Appearing
Real

What will facing your fear look like? Stepping into fear may involve articulating what you need or want, taking a chance on yourself in a way that you've never done before, leaving a bad situation or relationship, refusing to be a victim any longer, or applying for a job that you might not be fully qualified to do.

"I am fear. I am the menace that lurks in the path of life, never visible to the eye, but sharply felt in the heart. I am the father of despair, the brother of procrastination, the enemy of progress, and the tool of tyranny. Born of ignorance and nursed on misguided thought, I have darkened more hopes, stifled more ambitions, shattered more ideals and prevented more accomplishments than history could record.

Like the changing chameleon, I assume many disguises. I masquerade as caution. I am sometimes known as doubt or worry. But whatever I'm called, I'm still fear, the obstacle of achievement.

I know no master but one. Its name is understanding. I have no power but what the human mind gives me and I vanish completely when the light of understanding reveals the facts as they really are, for I am really nothing."

—Author unknown

Depersonalize the Situation

"This life is a test; it is only a test.
If it were a real life, you would receive
instructions on where to go and what to do."
~ Unknown

OFTEN THE CHALLENGES we are faced with are the result of decisions made by others, global economic trends, changing social norms, knee-jerk reactions and, yes, sometimes even the weather! Don't take it personally. The changes happening around you are affecting you, but they don't reflect your worth.

When a major change has come your way, particularly if you didn't want it, you may be tempted to conclude that this is *all about you.* You can lose perspective and begin to think that you are *jinxed* or *doomed* or a *loser.*

Put your experience in context. Look at what's happening in your industry, your company, community or social group that may be driving this change. Consider who else might be experiencing a similar situation.

Some people spend inordinate amounts of time trying to figure out *why* something has happened *to them.* For some, ruminating about why they were let go, got in a bad car accident or received a particular diagnosis, eats up so much energy that they stay stalled and find it difficult to begin the process of taking the next step.

There's value in debriefing any situation that happens to you. By debriefing a failed relationship, lost opportunity or health dilemma you increase your chances of preventing it from happening again. However, *ruminating* about the past and *debriefing* are different activities.

Ruminating means going over and over a situation, asking the, *what if* questions again and again. Debriefing involves asking questions that demand action and commitment. Debriefing also involves owning past choices, creating clarity and discovering possibilities.

Ruminating feels exhausting and demoralizing, is repetitious in nature – like hopping on a roller coaster and going round and round. It results in feeling guilty, fearful and resentful.

Debriefing feels energizing and hopeful. It involves progressive steps, identifying an issue and choosing an action. Debriefing will result in feelings of optimism and personal power. A good rule-of-thumb is to debrief your failures and celebrate your successes.

Take Charge of Your Own Morale

*"Sometimes I get the feeling that the whole world
is against me, but deep down I know
that's not true. Some of the smaller
countries are neutral."*
~ Robert Orben

PUTTING ANYONE ELSE in charge of keeping you positive disempowers you, so be your own one man/woman attitude factory. Often you hear people say things like, "He made me mad," or "She makes me feel guilty." Taken at face value these people are essentially saying that they aren't in charge of themselves—someone else is. And often, that someone is a complete stranger!

You have the ability to respond to all of the events in your life, in a manner of your own choosing. Although you don't control the world, you *do* control how you respond to what happens in your world. There are important differences between taking responsibility for everything and everyone, versus taking full responsibility for how you choose to react to events and the actions of others.

I'm advocating that you accept no responsibility for other people's actions and 100% responsibility for your own. That's right—100%. Keep the point of control for your life and your attitude with you. Don't give your power away. Taking full responsibility for your thoughts, feelings, choices and behaviors—and yes, even the situation you're in right now—sets the stage for you to begin to craft the life you want. When you see yourself as the victim of other people's dysfunctions, malicious intentions, blunders or bad Karma, you lessen your ability to clearly see and evaluate your options.

Taking full responsibility for yourself means not blaming others for what they're *doing to you;* it means evaluating your contribution in any event and looking for opportunities to interact in ways that affirm your dignity and the dignity of others. Exercising self-responsibility means avoiding *victim thinking*—the kind of thinking that causes you to blame others for your situation and end up feeling sorry for yourself.

What will it look and feel like for you to assume full responsibility for your emotions—all of them—the good, the bad and the ugly! There is power in owning your emotions, power that will fuel your change effort. Start today to be the one person in charge of your emotional health—and watch your confidence grow!

Meaning Making

"There is nothing in the world, I venture to say, that would so effectively help one to survive, even in the worst conditions, as the knowledge that there is meaning in one's life."
~ *Victor Frankyl*

THE LIBRARY OF Congress has described Victor Frankyl's book, *Man's Search for Meaning*, as one of the ten most influential books of the 20th century. Frankyl endured and survived four Nazi death camps, including Auschwitz from 1942–1945, while his wife, parents and other family members all died at the hands of their tormentors.

Frankyl developed his inciteful point of view largely as the result of his experiences as an inmate of the concentration camps. Like all who were imprisoned there, he witnessed extreme suffering and excruciating deaths. His observations of himself and his fellow prisoners led to the adoption of an attitude toward life that allowed him to survive the camps and, in his own words, "...find hope amid despair, beauty amid desolation and nobility amid depravity."

He asserts that humanity's primary motivational force in life is the search for meaning, even in the most dismal of circumstances. Survival, he came to believe, depended not merely on the daily struggle to stay alive, but on a sense of purpose, which in immediate terms meant a belief in the future. "The prisoner who had lost faith in the future—his future—was doomed," Frankyl said. "With the loss of belief in the future, he also lost his spiritual hold; he let himself decline and became subject to mental and physical decay."

51

What makes Frankyl's ideas so helpful to a would-be changer is that so often the need to change is the result of someone else's actions or decisions. When you've been caught by surprise, or by an event or decision someone has made that causes you to need to change, one of the first tasks is to make sense of it, for yourself. Often people's first thoughts are to decide if what has happened is a good thing or a bad thing—their worst nightmare or their greatest gift. If the change is dramatic or significant enough, people privately wonder, what does this mean about me, the people involved, life, safety, goodness, reality and God?

Don't wait for others to decide what the events in your life mean; you can choose their meaning. You can decide whether an event becomes the catalyst for change or the signal to stay put.

Consider the tragic events of 9/11. When the planes struck the twin towers in New York City, immediately the media began to spin meaning and individuals began to make meaning. The same set of circumstances came to mean completely different things to differing groups. Some used the event to confirm their existing belief in the innate goodness and resilience of the human spirit, while others saw it as tangible proof that the world was dangerous and full of evil. What did you think?

In your current set of circumstances, what meaning are you assigning the actions of those around you? Do you regard the events that are necessitating you to change as a gift or a curse? Is the spin you're putting on your state of affairs negative or life affirming?

The meaning we make of our experiences is individual and powerful. Choose well the meaning you ascribe to the events in your life.

Counting the Costs & Benefits of Change

"You can't wring your hands and roll up your shirtsleeves at the same time. Pick one."
~ *Pat Schroeder*

SANDY LOOKED FLUSHED—*almost excited—when she stepped in the door of my office that day. She had been counseling with me for some time and, because she had been away on a business trip, we hadn't met for a few weeks. For several months Sandy had worked on reviving her 15-year marriage. She hadn't been happy for a long time, and in the beginning had tried many things to get her husband's attention. When he didn't respond, she had become increasingly frustrated.*

She began the session by telling me about a wonderful man she had met and how being around him made her feel certain that her marriage was over. With a sense of urgency, she declared her decision to leave her husband – the sooner the better. As we explored her options, it was clear that she hadn't considered the full impact of a separation. She had three small children, a dog, a mortgage, rental property and an active extended family life, not to mention a husband who, through his own inattention, had no idea what was about to happen.

Unfortunately, Sandy's naiveté proved to be her downfall. Over the next few weeks, she spent more time with the new man in her life and almost no time planning for the big change coming in her life. She hadn't anticipated her husband's vindictive reaction, her in-law's

53

attempts to gain control over the children, her co-worker's disapproval of her blossoming romance or her children's grief. Most of all, she hadn't considered how she would feel when it came to actually leaving the family home and the safety of married life.

Within weeks of announcing her departure, she was living in a small apartment with only weekend access to her children. Her supervisor at work was talking to her about her performance and several of her closest friends had pulled away. She felt devastated and alone. Even the new man was having second thoughts.

Making life-altering changes like the one Sandy chose is never easy, but so much of what she experienced could have been avoided or minimized had she fully thought through the ripple effects of her choice. The one thing Sandy needed was the one thing she didn't have—a plan!

In business it's called a cost/benefit analysis—the calculation of the cost of a venture, squared off against the gains. The anticipated costs and benefits of any change plan can be grouped into four categories:

1. The *financial* costs/benefits

2. The *time* costs/benefits

3. *The personal* costs/benefits: physical, emotional and psychological

4. The *social* costs/benefits to family and friends

Calculating the expected cost and benefits of your change is an important step. Doing this now can inform and prepare you to remove obstacles *before* you begin. As we go along, take out your note pad and jot down any of the following that seem to apply to your particular change plan. For example:

- *If you lose weight,* you'll look and feel better, but you may have to spend money on some new clothes or avoid certain foods, people and places that are familiar to you.

- *If you change jobs,* you may make more money and enjoy greater status, but you may have to travel more, and accept more responsibility that translates into more time spent away from family and friends.

- *If you overcome your inability to speak in front of groups,* you'll enjoy a greater degree of comfort and be less stressed when presenting, but you may find that being asked to chair larger group meetings means that you will have to take on more responsibility.

The Financial Costs/Benefits

It's like the man said, "There are no free lunches." Just about any change plan will have some financial considerations. Your first cost was the purchase of this book, so make sure you account for that. You might also need to purchase learning materials, pay for classes, counseling and/or support group fees, compensate for time away from work or fund other activities to achieve your goal.

When I went to university as a mature student, it cost me everything I had at the time. I was a single mom raising three teenagers and caring for a dog. I had an old car, and even older clothes! I took out student loans, qualified for some grant money and worked at two part time jobs. I wore the same two pair of jeans for the years it took me to get through school, and on Friday nights, our big splurge was ordering pizza and renting a video. We certainly had everything we needed, but not much more. The financial cost was high, but the payoff for me and my children has been tremendous!

In some instances, the change may require you to sever ties with one or more family members—temporarily, or perhaps permanently—which could translate into a loss of financial help or support and, ultimately, could result in the loss of your inheritance.

In extreme cases, in which the change involves leaving a relationship or a job or deciding to relocate, the financial costs may include: loss of income for a time, job search fees, legal fees, lost property equity and the loss of shared financial resources. Of course, the financial costs should be manageable, and ultimately the change may yield financial gains. Here are some examples of financial costs/benefits:

- *Joining a gym to get fit* will have fees attached. However, being more physically fit can translate into lowered health costs, injury and accident costs.

- *Giving up an addiction* may initially cost you rehab and/or support group fees and perhaps even relocation costs, should you decide to move away from negative neighborhoods or environments. However, you may experience an increase in income due to your ability to maintain a higher level of performance on the job.

So, what are the financial costs/benefits associated with your change plans?

The Time Costs/Benefits

Running out of time is a common reason people cite for abandoning their plans for change. Don't let that be your excuse. Be realistic about the cost of the transition in minutes, hours, days, months or even years. For some, reaching their goal will take only a few days, for others it may take weeks, months or even years to succeed.

Various stages of the change process take differing amounts of time. It may take longer to get ready to make the change than it does to actually make the change. You may take several weeks to get ready to quit your job and begin the process of self-employment, but it may only take you ten minutes to actually hand in your resignation.

- *If your change plan involves other people*, it may only take a few weeks to decide on the course of action you want to take, and several more months to gather the support of those around you. Some changers find that making the move ultimately frees up time for them.

- *If you decide to stop gossiping at work,* you'll likely free up more time to be productive.
- *If you plan to stop being so driven to perfection,* you may have more time for kids, friends and fun!

IS IT TIME TO MAKE YOUR MOVE?

Often one's life stage is the motivator for making a change. People will say, "It's the perfect time because I'm old enough, young enough, tired or strong enough, angry enough, rich or poor enough, or socially connected or isolated enough. My community is supportive enough, the weather is right, the season is here, the kids are gone, the illness is over, and I'm in a new town/job/church/ community. I'm sick and tired of being sick and tired, and I'm ready to do this *right now!*"

Perhaps you dearly want to make this change, but feel you aren't old enough, educated enough, physically strong enough or financially able to make your move *right now.* Consider the time frame of your life in terms of your age, life stage, marital or parental status, career or physical health. Perhaps you've suffered a recent loss. When these situations are present, it may not be a good time to launch a change program. Waiting for a better time may be a wise decision. But, think about it—could there be something perfect about making this change *right now?*

The Personal Costs/Benefits

Often the enormity of the personal cost is what sends the uncommitted back to the starting block. Most changers will need to alter their daily routines to accommodate new activities for learning, journaling, exercising or meditation. If the change is significant, you'll undoubtedly need to grieve the losses and feel the regrets and sadness that accompany leaving old beliefs and behaviors behind. You may need to take a good long look at your self-talk, your core belief system and your working assumptions about relationships.

- *Changing jobs* may require you to challenge an old limiting belief about success, and who really deserves to be successful.

- *Increasing the intimacy in your significant relationships* may mean you will have to let go of the view you hold of how relationships are *supposed* to be, and make room for how they *really are.*

GOING PUBLIC

When you begin to do things differently, your life becomes more visible and transparent. People begin to notice you aren't the same and you don't treat yourself and/or them the same.

- *Taking classes* may make co-workers wonder about your motives. This could inspire both admiration and jealousy.

- *Making time for quiet reflection each day* might make family members nervous, wondering what you're thinking about and what you might do next.

The Social Costs/Benefits

We are social animals; we want to be liked, to belong, and to feel valued by those around us. People often feel okay about paying the price of change for themselves, but get derailed when those that they care about are affected.

Have you decided to stop being a people pleaser or the family's doormat? Maybe you vowed to be more assertive and speak up for yourself; only to find that people don't seem to like the *new* you as well as they did the former you.

Jackie was a mother of two small children, both were avid sports types and Jackie spent a great deal of her time chauffeuring her kids to practice, baking cookies for team fundraisers, distributing schedules and generally being everything to everyone. Over time she felt increasingly resentful at how much of her time and energy were being spent taking care of the team. She decided to make a change. She promised herself that she would only take on those responsibilities that she really loved doing.

She had always enjoyed the actual games, so she opted to bring the snacks to games and leave the rest of the responsibilities to the other parents. She felt good about her choice, and her husband and kids were supportive of her decision. The coach had a very different reaction. He had come to rely on Jackie, so he wasn't impressed with her new independence from the caretaker role. The other parents didn't like it either. They had enjoyed Jackie's efficiency at reminding them of game dates, team dues and generally picking up the administrative pieces for the team.

There were strong reactions to Jackie's new found freedom. Some parents stopped talking to her, while others refused to pick up her children after games—a gesture they'd been willing to do when Jackie was providing so much help to the team.

Sometimes, it's the things that we want to change the most that make us less popular with others.

- *If your new job means taking on a new schedule,* your kids might not approve because it means you can't pick them up from school anymore.

- *If your plan is to get fit,* your pizza buddies might think that you're a bore because you don't want to spend the whole evening eating with them.

A Special Word about Addictions

Addictions are personal habits that, over time, exact a hefty physical and social toll. Over the years, I've worked with a number of individuals who had made the decision to quit drinking or using illegal drugs. They chose the day, checked into a program, and quit. For many, the quitting itself represented a huge act of courage.

However, often the act of quitting is just the beginning of the hard work required by this life transformation. It's when people start to socialize again, without the aid of alcohol or mood altering drugs, that they can become discouraged. Their old friends, often innocently enough, are unsure about how to react to them *clean and sober*. For many in recovery their entire social persona was built around the addiction. Often friends and family members try subtle ways of inviting the recovering addict back into their old behaviors. If you feel this is happening, it may be necessary to break off friendships and/or family ties until the temptations to resume old behaviors is not as strong.

You don't change (or not change) to appease others. But it's important to face the reality that, the changes you want to make affect other people. Planning for the consequences – both positive and negative is just plain smart.

Carefully consider the costs of the change you're about to make. Take your time. Don't hurry this part. Make sure you've gained clarity about the potential costs and benefits for yourself and for those important to you. Then pay the price and keep moving forward.

The Cost of Not Changing

"Not to decide—is to decide."
~ *Unknown*

OFTEN, DECIDING *NOT* to make a change can carry a hefty price tag. Could deciding not to make your move now: decrease your life expectancy, affect your self-esteem and sense of accomplishment, or even dash your life-long dreams?

- *If you choose to put off learning to speak up for yourself,* you may lose the confidence and opportunities you now have, making the process even more difficult should you decide to change later.

- *If you decide to put off saving for retirement* until the kids are grown, you could find that your ability to save adequate funds is limited.

A Special Word to Parents

I think for those of you who are parents there is another very important question that begs a sober, thoughtful answer. What will the costs/benefits be to your children if you don't make this change now?

I've counseled many wonderful parents over the years whose strongest motivation for making difficult personal change was the welfare of their children. Sometimes, even when they weren't able to muster the courage to change for themselves, they did it for their children. In my view, there's no greater motivation.

61

- *If you're in an abusive relationship* and you just don't yet value yourself enough to leave, could you leave for the safety and well being of your children?

- *If you're trying to quit smoking,* think of the life-stealing damage of second hand smoke on your kids.

- *If you're fearful of going back to school* to prepare for a better paying position, consider how your children's lives will be enhanced as you face your fear and overcome it.

Whew! That was a challenge. Still with me? If you've made notes as you've been reading, you should have a list of the anticipated costs and benefits associated with this change. Forewarned is forearmed. Anticipating smart ways to cover the costs *before* you begin will save you time and will decrease the likelihood that the price tag of this change will derail your efforts.

Heal Your History:
Getting *Past* Your *Past*

"They spend their time
mostly looking forward to the past."
~ Unknown

FOR MANY PEOPLE in intense transitions, it's not the future that stands in their way, it's events in their past that drag them backward. For some self-changers, past failures and losses loom over the future like a threatening thunder cloud. Looking back only gives you a stiff neck. And that could make you cranky, less flexible and limit your forward vision.

The past is the past. It happened. It's over. Acknowledge it—all of it. If it has been long and bad—admit that to yourself. If it was wonderful and now it's over—admit that. If you saw this coming a long time ago and chose to ignore it—forgive yourself. If good friends warned you that this would happen—remind yourself that you can count on these wise advisors more than you thought. If this is the second, third, or 100th time this same negative thing has happened—resolve to make this the last time.

Dragging the baggage of past relationships, jobs, financial entanglements, decisions or even past glories and dreams can weigh down the most hearty change traveler. Refuse to be labeled or burdened by what you used to feel or how someone used to treat you, how you once behaved, or what you thought things would be like. Now is what counts!

Honoring The Past

Do you need to thank yourself for having adopted the behavior that you now want to change? Think about it. There's a good chance that the behavior or thought pattern that you now want to change was actually helpful to you at one time. Here are some examples of how people learned a behavior when they were young, only to find that in adulthood it didn't work any more.

- *As an adolescent, you over ate* to compensate for feeling second best in the family. Now you're uncomfortable with the extra weight and want to get fit.

- *You started drinking as a way of relaxing* before social gatherings. It helped you to feel calmer, more in control and less shy. Now you can't go to a party without a drink at home first.

- *When you were a child, you learned to keep your mouth shut* to keep your angry parent from lashing out at you. Years later, you have a hard time speaking up for yourself, even when you want to.

To honor your past is to review why you chose those behaviors, beliefs or reactions in the first place. You may find it helpful to engage in a ritual or ceremony to mark the end of how things *used to be*.

Example:

I knew a woman who had adopted the childhood behavior of being inappropriate and loud to gain her considerably dysfunctional parents' attention. Always capturing center stage at family functions was literally the only way she was ever seen or heard. As an adult her behavior was becoming increasingly problematic as she was attempting to move up the corporate ladder, and her domineering manner had showed up in her performance reviews several times. She had committed herself to changing how she was reacting in stressful situations and, as a first step, created a little ceremony for herself to say good bye to her old behavior.

With my encouragement she created a certificate of appreciation for herself, thanking herself for being clever enough to figure out early how to be seen and heard by inattentive parents. Then she went to her office after hours when no one was there, slipped into the board room and stood at the head of the table, and ceremoniously awarded herself the certificate. She held it for a few moments, remembering how her loud, overbearing ways had helped her survive. Then she quietly folded the certificate and tucked it into a secret pocket in her briefcase. As she left the boardroom, she felt free and ready to begin to act more in line with her adult self.

Sound funny? It's amazing how wonderfully liberating a ritual or ceremony like this can be. Try it. Think of your goal. Are there behaviors that you will need to change to accomplish this goal? How have these old behaviors, and ways of being in the world, been serving you? What behaviors or choices in your past do you deserve credit for? What will you need to do instead?

Necessary Losses

The Dakini Speaks

My friends, let's grow up.
Let's stop pretending we don't know the deal here.
Or if we truly haven't noticed, let's wake up and notice.
Look: everything that can be lost—will be lost.
It's simple—how could we have missed it for so long?
Let's grieve our losses fully, like ripe human beings.
But, please, let's not be so shocked by them.
Let's not act so betrayed.
As though life had broken her secret promise to us.
Impermanence is life's only promise to us.
And she keeps it with ruthless impeccability…

~ Jennifer Weldwood

SO HOW WILL you tackle the task of letting go? What does letting go in a healthy way look and feel like? I've been asked that question many times. An important step in the letting go phase of the change process is honoring past decisions and behaviors *before* moving away from them.

I was the kind of little girl who dreamed of the day I'd get married. I spent inordinate amounts of time fantasizing about the white dress, the *tall, dark and handsome* man and of course, the *happily ever after*. Deeply embedded in my psyche was the romantic notion of *wife*—the most important role I would ever fill. However, after 17 years of trying to contort the reality of my marriage to fit the fantasy picture in my head, I finally admitted defeat. And while I didn't miss the man—I really missed the role. Letting go of my dreams of being the consummate wife, housekeeper and companion was gut wrenching and horrible. I felt like I was jumping off a very steep cliff, with no parachute and no idea what I would find when I hit the bottom. I had thought of myself as someone's *better half* for most of my adult life, and my identity was completely re-ordered by the change. This *big, fat change* necessitated my letting go of tightly-held dreams, social standing, financial stability, a house, *stuff* and, for a while, the daily presence of one of my children.

Are you holding on to something that's preventing you from grabbing on to your dreams? Some of the most painful losses we may have to bear are self-image losses—when we see ourselves as the family favorite, a *good girl* or the one who can do anything. Maybe being the family hero has been a role for which you've received kudos. To stop looking after everyone else now will mean losing status.

With any major change there are necessary losses; those things we must let go of in order to move ahead. Clinging to old ideas, behaviors, hurts and experiences will keep you mired in the past. Whatever the loss—feel it fully, say good-bye and boldly step forward.

Challenge Your Beliefs

"Man is what he believes."
~ Anton Chekhov

UNLESS YOUR CORE beliefs change—nothing changes. Permanently altering behavior requires a shift in thinking. Albert Einstein said that you couldn't solve a problem with the same mindset that created it. To change what you feel and do, you must first understand what's in your mind—specifically, what's in your belief system. You must understand how your belief system works, and how to make it work for you.

What is a belief system? Our beliefs are our personal blueprints for daily living. Everything we think, feel and do is driven by our basic beliefs about ourselves, others and the world around us. Your beliefs are your *should* and *ought to* values and mental schemas. Beliefs fuel your mental engine, dictate your feelings and behaviors and provide the foundation for how you approach your world—and they are powerful!

We form our belief systems in childhood and act them out in adulthood. Children watch what happens around them and then draw conclusions about what it all means. These childhood conclusions become adult belief systems.

The good news is that your beliefs are just beliefs. They are the sense that you made of the world when you were young – they're not *you*.

People often find that when they get to the action phase of the change process, they run headlong into old limiting beliefs that hold them back. Here are some examples of limiting beliefs in action:

- *You've decided to become more assertive and speak up for yourself in work situations,* yet every time you try, your heart races and you feel like you're a child again, afraid of getting scolded for asking for what you want.

- *You're trying to stop using alcohol as a way to handle your feelings,* but when you get really frustrated, you find yourself remembering all of the negative things that your dad used to say about you, and it makes you want a drink.

These types of physical and emotional reactions can signal that you're facing an old belief about yourself, others or the situation, that's stopping you from moving forward. This is especially true when you encounter fear. When an anticipated change creates a fearful reaction, you can be assured that there's a belief in place telling you that it's dangerous to do what you're trying to do, say what you're about to say, or feel what you're actually feeling.

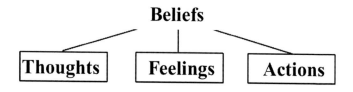

The beauty of belief systems is that they're flexible. You can re-decide and choose again what to believe about a situation, yourself or other people. Remember: your beliefs are just beliefs. They're the sense that you made of the world when you were young—they're not necessarily *you*. The largest part of the work people do in therapy is to re-evaluate their belief systems; they decide from an adult perspective which beliefs to hold on to and which ones to discard or modify.

Distorted Realities—Beliefs That Bind

Through the pioneering work of Eric Erickson, Carl Jung and other human psychology practitioners, we know that our basic beliefs are in place by about age 5-7. By the time we reach young adulthood our beliefs are largely unconscious and are operating out of our awareness; our childhood beliefs act much like a computer operating system—directing how we think, feel, make decisions and respond. Unless our beliefs are mindfully re-examined, they remain unchallenged dictators of our daily behavior. The good news is that when carefully inspected and challenged, your beliefs, and the behaviors that accompany them, can be changed.

There are many reasons why children form inaccurate and limiting belief systems.

- Children have a limited set of experiences from which to design the belief systems that eventually govern their adult lives. If mom and dad say it, do it or believe it – it's gospel.

- Children are magical thinkers; they believe Santa Claus makes it to every chimney in the world in one night!

- Children see the world in black and white terms; they think that the population is made up of the good guys and the bad guys. Children lack the mental and/or emotional maturity to sift through the shades of gray in people's behavior. They don't yet understand that most people are capable of an array of both positive and negative behaviors.

- Children are egocentric. Because of their limited experiences, and their natural need for continuous love and protection, they see their

71

world from the vantage point of need, vulnerability and dependency.

Children craft their belief systems by:

- noticing their own feelings and responses, and assigning meaning.

- observing other people and events, then drawing conclusions.

- being told directly about themselves, others and the meaning of events.

Example:

- *Mom and dad attend all of their daughter's soccer games,* cheering her on whether she wins or loses.

The little girl concludes that she's special and important in her parents' lives.

- *Mother is depressed,* and so spends most of her day crying and looking to her child for comfort. Her small son decides it's his job to take care of mom and make her feel better.

You can see how the children in these examples have come to some definite conclusions about life—some positive and life affirming—some negative and life limiting. After working with hundreds of people making personal change, I've realized that there's no predicting what conclusions children will come to in response to a set of events or experiences. Although one would think that negative events would produce negative conclusions and conversely positive events would produce positive conclusions—and it's often that way—it's not always that predictable. I've often been told of negative events that have resulted in children making strong and positive decisions about themselves, while seemingly positive circumstances have produced a pessimistic and limiting belief.

The beliefs people form through the eyes and experiences of a child are often irrational, exaggerated and/or simply incorrect.

- *Four year-old Susan watches her mom and dad* hovering over the table at tax time with worried looks. She wonders if the mess that she made earlier in the day is causing them this misery.

- *Bobby's little sister dies suddenly* and at the funeral he overhears the relatives talking about how his mother will *never be the same again*. He decides that his mother is now fragile and he needs to take care of her.

- *Paula's parents win a new car in a local lottery* and when the car is delivered her dad picks her up, swings her around and says she's his *lucky charm*. Paula decides that she's magic and can do anything, anywhere, for anyone!

Children also form their belief systems by modeling others. The *little ducks do what big ducks do*. Because children want to make sense of their world, and the big people in it, they watch, listen and emulate whenever possible.

- *Dad comes home from work tired.* Mom gives him a hug, brings him slippers and tells him to relax, saying that supper will be ready soon. The little girls in the family decide it's up to mommies (women) to care for daddies (men). The little boys in the family decide that men are important and that wives should take care of them.

- *A waitress brings the wrong order* and Uncle Fred criticizes her loudly, saying, "She's just a stupid waitress—no wonder she got it wrong." The children at the table watch with interest and decide that service people can be spoken to disrespectfully.

Now, fast forward to adulthood. As adults, we have the advantage of being able to gather information about ourselves from friends, family, co-workers, internet buddies, or neighbors.

73

We can read books, watch movies or attend events – all resources that give us an opportunity to think about ourselves in light of thousands of other people's experiences.

Here's a partial list of some commonly held negative beliefs:

- I must please all the people all the time—or die trying.
- Things must go the way I want them to—or I won't be okay.
- I must be good at everything I do—or I shouldn't even try.
- If I feel sad, mad or lonely, I won't be able to handle it.
- I am what people have told me I am.
- I'm only capable of being what my parents were.
- It's disrespectful and wrong for me to draw attention to myself.
- It's not okay for me to make a mistake. If I do, I should hide or deny it.
- I am my thoughts.
- I am my body.
- If things are going well—something bad is about to happen.
- It's not smart to take a risk.
- People are either good or bad.
- Life is against me.

Some positive beliefs are:

- I can do anything I set my mind to.
- Most people are good and can be trusted.
- I deserve love and respect.
- I can change whatever I want to change.
- I'm in charge of my own life.
- I'm in charge of my own emotions

- I'm blessed.
- I like myself.
- I have an important purpose for being on the planet.
- I'm competent.
- I can learn.
- People like me.
- I am more than any one thing I've done or said.
- Even though my original family treated me badly, I will love and be loved.
- My past is past.

Now it's time for you to go to work on your own limiting beliefs. What belief do you keep running up against? Write down your beliefs in clear and simple statements like the ones above.

When you've got a good picture of what the old belief is, *write the antidote to it.* Just like a snake bite requires an antidote, think of old, limiting beliefs as poison, in need of an antidote. Design the antidote for each of the limiting beliefs that threaten to hold you back in your change process. If you need help with this exercise, ask a trusted friend to review your list of limiting beliefs. You may be amazed to learn how different your *realities* look to them. Your friend has grown up with a completely different set of beliefs and will find some of your *hard and fast* truths to be ridiculous, maybe even laughable.

I remember the time I remarked to a friend that I couldn't go to university because I was too old. I was 38 at the time. Many times I had heard people say that, "Life is over at 40." And I had believed them. My friend found that belief simply laughable. Yes, she laughed at what I had held as truth! I had come to believe that all the really good stuff, learning included, had to happen before 40 years of age, or it would never happen. It was refreshing, and a little embarrassing, to see my childhood belief held up to the light of day. So, go ahead, risk taking-in some new information.

Here are some examples of old beliefs and their antidotes.

Old Belief:

"I've been heavy since I was 10. I've tried to diet before and failed. This time will be just like all the rest."

Antidote:

"I'm more prepared now to make good choices about how to design a successful weight loss program."

Old Belief:

"My dad was an alcoholic. I'm just like he was. He couldn't stay sober, and neither can I."

Antidote:

"I'm not my dad. I can make different choices."

Old Belief:

"No one in my family has ever graduated from university. I'm kidding myself to think that I can."

Antidote:

"I can be part of my family and still be different from them. I can succeed, even though others haven't."

Designing antidotes to the limiting beliefs of childhood helps you heal the past and move forward. Take your time with this exercise. It just may be the one that frees you to change.

When you've articulated your new beliefs, post them where you can see them often. A powerful way to embed a new belief is to look around in the world for confirmation —read articles and stories that support your new way of seeing the world. Spend time with people who share your new perspective. Watch how quickly you can replace old, limiting beliefs with new, empowering ones.

Thought Traps
that Block Change

"It's time for thinking people to think."
~ Maya Angelou

THERE ARE SEVEN types of Thought Traps, or erroneous ways of thinking, that children fall prey to when trying to make sense of their world. Often these ways of reasoning stay with people throughout life, serving to reinforce how they continue to feel about themselves—and their ability to change. Let's look first at how thought traps show up in childhood and then how, if not corrected, they continue to operate in adulthood.

1. All or Nothing Thinking

Remember that children think in black and white terms. They don't have the cognitive maturity to do otherwise.

- *Six-year-old Sam didn't get a star on his artwork.* The teacher said it was too messy and that he should try again. He tells himself he just can't do art, and that he's just too dumb to be in school.

- *Benjamin waited all morning for his best friend to ask him to play,* but the friend never called. He told his mother that his friend was a mean kid, and that he didn't like him anymore. Benjamin declared he never wanted to see his friend again.

All or Nothing Thinking in Adulthood

- *Bill is passed over for a promotion* because he lacked the necessary skills. Bill tells himself he's a complete loser and that he'll never get promoted.

- *Sandra's husband says he's not fond of the outfit she's chosen* for the dinner party. She runs out of the room crying and tells herself that her husband doesn't love her any more.

Is there any *all or nothing thinking* shadowing your change efforts?

2. Jumping to Conclusions

Children lack the ability to see the bigger picture that would allow them to put situations into a more reasonable context. Children often take one event and extrapolate it to everything.

- *Karl sees his friends going out to recess laughing and whispering to each other.* No one asked him to come along. He thinks that they're talking about him and that they will probably exclude him from their plans for the game after school that day.

Jumping to Conclusions in Adulthood

- *Rick comes home late from work and his wife's car isn't in the driveway as it usually is.* He remembers that she was going to a conference that day and immediately feels sad. He tells himself that she's more interested in her career than she is in him, and that this is probably the first of many lonely nights for him.

3. Personalization—It's all about Me

Children under 11 years of age see themselves as the center of the universe, and everything and everyone as having some connection to them and their behavior. As a result, whenever events happen—positive or negative—they attribute it to something they have said or done. Personalizing is a dangerous thought trap when you're trying to make changes. If you think everyone's behavior is related to what you do or say, you'll be constantly dipping and dodging to avoid hurting feelings and inconveniencing others. You may find yourself trying to *please all the people all the time*—without success.

- *Kevin wished his baby sister would go away.* He thinks life was better before she was born. When his sister gets sick, he feels guilty, thinking that he caused her to become sick.

Personalization in Adulthood

- *Ellen really likes the guy she's been dating.* When he doesn't call for a week, she thinks back over their past few dates, searching for what she did that caused him to pull away.

4. Over Generalizing

This term refers to the habit of seeing *one* event or response dictating *all* future things.

- *Six-year-old Sally is shopping with her mother* and asks if she can have new shoes. Her mother says *no.* Sally lowers her head and mutters that, she'll probably never get anything new again.

Over Generalizing In Adulthood

- *Margaret is applying for a job after staying home for several years.* She's sent out four resumes and hasn't yet received a response. She begins to tell herself that she'll probably never get a job —and that companies just don't want women who've been out of the workforce as long as she has.

5. Emotional Reasoning

You *feel* it, so it must be true. Emotional reasoning is a powerful thought trap that can get in the way of more rational reasoning when you're trying to make changes. Feelings are feelings. Reality is often something quite different.

- *Jack is afraid to go into his room* because he has just watched a scary movie and is sure that there are monsters lurking under his bed.

Emotional Reasoning in Adulthood

- *Lately, Helen has been sensing that her husband just doesn't love her any more.* Although he behaves the same way as he always has, and he assures her he still loves her, she keeps thinking something is wrong.

6. Minimizing/Magnifying

Minimizing and magnifying are two sides of the same coin. This happens when a person understates or overstates a feeling, situation or response due to fear, lack of information or a distorted sense of reality.

- *The teacher chooses Eric to erase the whiteboards.* Eric decides he's the teacher's pet and can boss all the other kids around.

Minimizing/Magnifying in Adulthood

- *Penny has been on an exercise program for three weeks* and has lost two pounds. She tells her friends that the program isn't working, and that she's going to quit because she *hasn't lost anything.*

7. Mind Reading

Mind reading refers to the act of making assumptions about other people's thoughts, feelings and behaviors without checking the evidence.

- *Jimmy walks past a group of kids* and notices that one of the girls turns away as he goes by. He thinks, "I just know she hates me."

Mind Reading in Adulthood

- *Sandra interviews with a prospective employer* and when she leaves thinks to herself, "I could tell he thought I was stupid."

Are thought traps getting in your way? Some of these common thought traps may have been demonstrated to you in your family, neighborhood or at school. You don't have to be stopped by these pesky stumbling blocks. You can challenge how you think about a situation and decide on a more accurate and productive way of dealing with it.

Which thinking trap is the most problematic for you right now? Write out clear statements about it, distilled into simple sentences. Then challenge them. Are these statements true? When did you begin to believe this? Who else in your family or among your friends believes this same thing? By examining the seven Thought Traps you'll gain clarity on how you may be trapped, and especially how this erroneous thinking is holding you back from making the changes you want.

The Power of Decision

"While we are postponing, life speeds by."
~ *Seneca (3BC - 65AD)*

THERE'S NO SUBSTITUTE for a powerful decision. Races have been won, businesses built, illnesses overcome and lives changed forever, because someone decided to make it happen.

Jenny was born in 1956 with a cleft pallet. In those days, the surgery for birth defects was still somewhat unsophisticated and she was left with a fairly visible scar and a lisp. The other kids teased her at school and she learned at an early age not to accept any assignments that might require her to make a presentation to the class. Although she had always dreamed of working with special needs children, she chose not to go to university to get the qualifications that would have allowed her to fulfill her dream.

Over the years she had one mediocre administration job after another, always feeling that what she really wanted to do was out of reach because of her view of her limitations. On a rainy afternoon in 1994, she was driving home from work and was hit head on by a drunk driver. Her car was totaled and she spent six weeks in hospital. With plenty of time on her hands, and a new found appreciation of the life she was spared, she made a decision – a big one. She was going to do whatever it took to prepare herself to follow her life's dream. When she left the hospital, she applied, and was accepted, to university,

secured student loans, quit her job and moved into a friend's
apartment. The rest, as they say, is history.

Today you'll find Jenny at one of Toronto's finest day care facilities, surrounded by playful toddlers who've been diagnosed with a variety of challenges. Jenny has shared her story with hundreds of people and considers herself to be a walking testimony to the power of making a decision.

On Your Mark
Review

IT'S TIME FOR a quick review. As you answer the questions below, reflect on how far you've come. Look for early wins and points of growth so far. Honestly allow yourself to see areas where you still have some work to do. You needn't be perfect to move on. Just do a candid review and prepare yourself for the next exciting steps.

Here's your checklist:

1. Which of the 7 Naked Truths do you need to remember most?
2. Have you chosen and clarified your goal?
3. Are you expecting success?
4. What will help you stay focused?
5. How will you handle your fear about this process?
6. Have you depersonalized the situation, if appropriate?
7. Who is in charge of your morale?
8. What will it mean to you when you have accomplished this goal?
9. Have you thoroughly documented the costs associated with accomplishing your goals?
10. Are you healing your history as you go?
11. How can you honor the past and still move on?
12. What losses will this change require of you?

13. Have you done a review of the core beliefs that affect your progress?

14. Have you planned ways to avoid the thought traps?

If you've completed all of these exercises, you're now ready to move on to the *Get Set* section of this book. You'll want to refer to the ideas in this section often as they will come to act as the foundation of your change process.

Get Set

Autobiography in Five Short Chapters
By Portia Nelson

Chapter I

I walk down the street.
There is a deep hole in the sidewalk.
I fall in.
I am lost. I am helpless.
It isn't my fault.
It takes me forever to find a way out.

Chapter II

I walk down the same street.
There is a deep hole in the sidewalk.
I pretend I don't see it.
I fall in again.
I can't believe I am in the same place.
But, it isn't my fault.
It still takes a long time to get out.

Chapter III

I walk down the same street.
There is a deep hole in the sidewalk.
I see it is there.
I still fall in. It's a habit.
My eyes are open.
I know where I am.
It is my fault.
I get out immediately.

Chapter IV

I walk down the same street.
There is a deep hole in the sidewalk.
I walk around it.

Chapter V

I walk down another street.

Just in Time

When you come to the edge of all the light,
and you know you're about to step off
into the darkness of the unknown,
faith is knowing that
one of two things will happen.
There will be something solid to stand on,
or you will be taught how to fly.
~ Author unknown

DURING THE EARLY transitions in my life I often thought that I didn't have the will, ideas, friends, strength, support, information, or answers I *really* needed to succeed. I would spend hours wishing for better opportunities, clearer direction, the *right* people or clues to appear to show me what to do and how to do it.

For much of my life I believed I just didn't have the money to change. I would listen to the stories of other people making job changes, going back to school, losing weight, or starting over and I would think, "Sure. I'd do that too, if I had *their* money."

I often found myself thinking that the reason I was in this mess in the first place was that somehow I'd been short-changed, victimized or led astray and that in order to find my way out, I needed *something else*—something that I didn't yet possess, and would probably never have.

Now I know differently. I've learned that resources, ideas and opportunities in life arrive *just in time*. On so many occasions, what I've needed has often come right before I've needed it. Let me explain it another way. In the past, assembly plants bought large amounts of inventory and then housed their stock in large warehouses or yards and when they needed materials, someone brought them by forklift to the assembly line. Now, manufacturers keep a close watch on the quantities that they need, and when they need more they purchase and schedule the arrival of supplies *just in time* to be put on the assembly line. This approach eliminates the costly warehousing of inventory. The universe seems to operate in the same way. We seem to get just what we need, and often no more than that, just before we really need it.

Take note... and heart. Everything you need is already with you—right here, right now. It's the simple truth.

We seem to get what we need, just when we need it, and not a moment sooner. During my times of intense change, when I needed *it* the most, and was sure *it* wasn't coming, *it* happened; the right person, the perfect job offer, a great idea, unexpected money, an offer of help, advice, insight, wisdom, clarity, courage, 'stuff', a great suggestion and/or a burst of energy—all just in the nick of time.

If you want to see all the answers before you begin, you'll never begin. If you need to know exactly what your world will be like before making your move, you'll never move. Believe it before you see it; like turning on a light switch, *trust* that it's going to be there. I don't know why it works this way, but it does. I've learned to trust this phenomenal life gift and expect it. But you have to know where to look. Not for a minute am I suggesting that you just sit back and wait for the cosmos to make a house call with all the goods. But what I am suggesting is that you keep moving—making decisions, taking steps in the direction that you want to go; anticipating that what you need will be there when you need it.

In order to work with the universe and not against it, you'll need to sharpen a few skills. The first one is listening. You'll need to listen—*really* listen to what people around you are saying and what they're offering.

The truth comes in many forms during a transition. Many times, the answer or insight for which I'd been searching, was given to me in someone's simple comment that I'd brushed off. Only later did I realize the profound value in what they were saying. This has happened so many times that now, when someone is speaking to me, I listen as intently as I can. By actively listening, I've been given business leads, money saving tips, feedback on personal areas of needed growth, novel approaches to a chronic problem, a song that soothes, vital health information, important reminders and much, much more.

Case in point: *When I was newly separated, I needed two things: time with my kids and a place where I could process what had happened. But I was broke and in university full time. I needed to work and couldn't afford therapy. However, when finances were at their worst and I thought I'd have to quit school, I got a job—make that two jobs—just in time! One job was coordinating a Friday night kids program in my local town. My children were 13 and 15 years-old, so every Friday night I got paid to play with a great group of kids, including my own!*

My second job was organizing support groups for people going through separation and divorce. It was my job to open the room, make the coffee and introduce the speaker. Perfect or what? I'd sit in those meetings and listen to the advice and experiences of the participants. I'd pick up brochures and get ideas for coping with the legal, financial, emotional and family issues that separation brings, all the while getting paid to be there.

If you learn to relax and trust the process, you will discover that you have hidden strengths and talents that will surface—just in time. You'll recognize options that were out of your sight before. You'll develop sources of support, from people who weren't in your life before, or those whom you knew, but didn't realize could help you.

Whispers, taps, slaps and bombs

I've learned that when things are changing, help comes to us in the most unusual and interesting ways. Let me explain.

When change is *in the wind*, our first awareness of it may come in a *whisper*—a gentle warning voice, saying, "Hey, look at that", or "Did you hear what she just said." Some of the whispers I've heard, but didn't understand until much later, came in the form of a sense that something was wrong—a fleeting look passing across someone's face that made me wonder. Life's whispers are important clues, urging us to pay attention to what just happened, is about to happen or what is changing.

> *"None of us will ever accomplish anything excellent or commanding except when he listens to this whisper which is heard by him alone."*
>
> - Ralph Waldo Emerson

If we don't pay attention to the whispers, the universe will step closer and decide to show us what's going on in a more emphatic way. After unheeded whispers, often comes a 'tap on the shoulder'—a tap designed to get our attention in a gentle, but more direct way. Some of the taps I've received over the years have included a physical twitch or pain, a comment from a friend that struck me as odd, a song that reminded me how I used to feel about something that's beginning to feel bad. When taps are ignored, a sudden and often painful *slap* often comes next.

A *slap* is often a sudden realization that something is very wrong. A slap could come in the form of information from a friend or enemy that runs counter to what you've always thought or believed, a glance in the mirror that reveals neglect of your body or health, or reading something from a book or poem that gives you a sick feeling in your stomach. If we don't take notice when we're smacked by life, then a *bomb* may be the next thing we encounter.

A *bomb* is characterized by a serious life-altering event —a partner abruptly leaves, you have an accident, lose a job or find yourself losing your composure and saying and doing things you never thought you'd say or do.

My advice is to listen to the whispers. *Get* what your world is trying to tell you the first time. Don't ignore incoming information, feelings and intuition. If someone or something is tapping you on the shoulder, pay attention. Figure out the message. If you've just been slapped with something in your life, look around your environment and ask questions. Something is trying to get your attention. And if you've just had a bomb go off in your life—hold on! It likely won't get any worse than this, *if* you take the time to deal with it *now*.

Another great resource for recognizing that what you really need is right *here* and *now*, comes from the people in your life. Think back to a time when you were at a crossroad—a time when you were choosing between two or more options. What and who was around you?

This lovely piece by Lois Cheney says it all about the people in our lives and how they shape us.

Bits and pieces
Bits and pieces

People.
People important to you.
People unimportant to you cross your life, touch it with love
and carelessness, and move on.
There are people who leave you and you breathe a sigh of
relief and wonder why you ever came into contact with them.
There are people who leave you and you breathe a sigh of
remorse and wonder why they had to go away and leave such
a gaping hole.
Children leave parents; friends leave friends. Acquaintances
move on. People change homes. People grow apart. Enemies
hate and move on. Friends love and move on. You think on
the many that have moved into your hazy memory. You look
on those present and wonder.

95

I believe in God's master plan in lives. He moves people in and out of each other's lives; each leaves his mark on the other. You find you're made up of the bits and pieces of all who ever touched your life, and you're more because of it, and you would be less if they had not touched you.
Pray that you accept the bits and pieces in humility and wonder and never question and never regret.

Bits and pieces
Bits and pieces

Who are the people in your life right now? What could they teach you, give to you or require of you that will make this time of transition clearer, smoother, more fun or meaningful?

The Pain/ Pleasure Principle

"Sometimes it's got to get worse before it gets better. Sometimes it's not until the muck and mire are so deep, so thick, that we realize there has got to be a change."
~ Iyanla Vanzant

CONVENTIONAL WISDOM SAYS that if you're going to be successful at making a significant change in your personal or professional life, it will be for one of two reasons: either it's just too painful to stay in your current situation, or the rewards for making the change are so promising that you are willing to endure some pain to achieve those rewards.

What are your reasons for wanting to make this change (the Pleasure) and reasons you don't want to (the Pain)?

I've got some good news for you about those annoying downsides to the change you want to make. James O. Prochaska, PhD., John C. Norcross, PhD. and Carlo C. Diclement, PhD., well-known researchers in the field of change, have spent years studying how successful self-changers overcome their perceptions of the negative aspects of making a change. Prochaska and his group studied several thousand people and found that when successful self-changers make a Pain/Pleasure (or pro/con) list, there is roughly a 10% ratio difference between the reasons they list for wanting to make the change and their reasons for not wanting to make the effort.

Their theory goes something like this; when people are just entertaining (Pre-Contemplation) a change, their reasons for not taking action are greater than their reasons for moving ahead, and seem more important to them. As they move into what I call the Insight phase (Contemplation) their Pain/ Pleasure lists become more evenly weighted. But as people move into the Action phase of their change plan, their reasons for wanting to make the change (the Pleasures) become more important and begin to edge out the more negative aspects (The Pain) of the process.

The good news for you is that if you want to move from just *thinking* about making a change to actually *doing it*—you can, and taking a good look at your Pain list is the place to start. Look hard at your Pain list. Do you really want these things to hold you back? Do you want these reasons/excuses to be what dominates your thinking now? Or would you rather fill your life with the feelings and rewards showcased on your Pleasure list?

Try this simple, time tested approach:

First, draw a line down the middle of a piece of lined paper (like the one on the following page) and write **Pleasure** on the top of one side and **Pain** on the top of the other. On the Pleasure side of the paper, list the reasons you want to make the change. These reasons should be put into two categories: *Pleasure* for *Self* and *Pleasure* for *Others*. This list will include all the reasons you want or need to make the change – your new look, more freedom, increased self-esteem, career advancement – and all those wonderful outcomes that you hope will be yours. This list will become your constant companion on your way to your goal, so include everything.

Pleasure		Pain	
Self	**Others**	**Self**	**Others**

For the Pain list, write down all those things associated with your change that you'll have to risk, give up, stop doing, lose out on, or learn to do. Also summarize all of the sacrifices your family and friends will have to make for you to be different.

Now, look at your lists. Which is the longest, most detailed or fullest? If your Pleasure list is at least 10% longer or fuller than your Pain list, you're ready for action. If your Pain list is longer and more detailed, you still have some work to do. Keep looking for more reasons to make the change. Perhaps you can talk to family and friends. The people close to you can often give you ideas about why making this change will be helpful, healthy, positive and life affirming, as well as provide you with insights into the challenges you may have overlooked. Your Pain and Pleasure list is the place to spend time thinking through what's really motivating you.

The Balancing Act

From the day we arrive on the planet
And blinking, step into the sun,
There's more to be seen than can ever be seen
More to do than can ever be done.
In the circle of life
It's the wheel of fortune
It's the leap of faith
It's the band of hope
Till we find our place
On the path unwinding
In the circle, the circle of life.
~ Elton John

OUR NATURAL NEED to grow and become all that we can be is another very strong motivating force for change. I think that it's unnatural not to change, grow, and choose to take another path, disrupt routines and transform ourselves.

Just as young children are always growing, learning new skills and leaving old ways behind, I believe it's natural to continue to transform over a lifetime. Clinging to old ways, outdated routines, and parental behavior models and self-defeating patterns is unhealthy and unnatural.

Life stage is an important consideration when thinking about where the change fits. Are you just entering the young adult phase of maturation where this change reflects your need to move to the next phase of adulthood? Or are you in the *empty nest* phase of your life, anticipating your emerging independence from the rigors of childrearing?

What kind of change are you making, where does your change fit on the wheel that follows?

There may be some overlap between areas. For instance, changing careers may necessitate returning to school (intellectual) and securing student loans (financial).

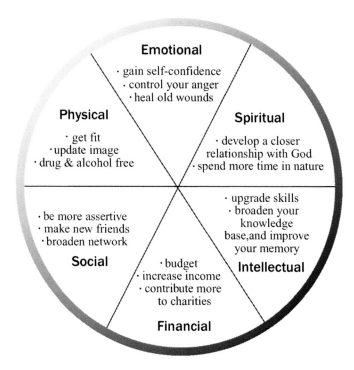

It can be easy to slip out of balance. Some people are intellectually accomplished, but physically out of balance. Others are socially adept, but spiritually bankrupt. Still others spend a great deal of time setting career goals, but never think to map out personal goals. Some of the things people choose to change in their lives are highlighted in the wheel above. In which area of your life do you want to grow? Which areas of your life will your change effort affect?

What's Motivating You?

"He who hesitates is a damned fool."
~ *Mae West*

EXAMINING YOUR MOTIVATIONS for wanting to make a change is a key step in preparing for, and being successful at making a major change. Why do you really want to do this? What dream, desire or necessity will it fill in your life? Here are some more ways to look at what is really motivating you.

Sometimes there's a fine line between what we need and what we want and, often they're *very* different things.

- *I may want a better paying job,* but if I don't really *need* the money, I may lack the motivation to do the work to get a new position.

- *I may want to stop drinking*, but I will be a lot more serious about it if I'm convinced I *need* to quit.

There's nothing wrong—and everything right—about really, really *wanting* things to change. But few people pull out all the stops to achieve their goals unless they're also convinced that they *need* to change.

On the next page is the Need/Want Model of Motivation that I've designed to help you get clearer about whether you need *or* want, or need *and* want to make this change. Read the statements below the diagram to see where your thoughts fit.

103

Want to/ **Don't Need to**	**Want to/** **Need to**
Don't Need to/ **Don't Want to**	**Need to/** **Don't Want to**

Change Ready ↑

← *Not Change Ready*

Completing the statements below will help you gain clarity about your determination to achieve your goal.

I Need It / I Want It:

- I need to be different in this way so I can......
- I need to accomplish this goal so I will......
- I need to be able to do this so others will......
- I need to know that I can make this change so...... and/or
- I want to be different in this way so I can......
- I want to accomplish this goal so I will......
- I want to be able to do this so that others will......
- I want to know that I can make this change so ......

I Don't Need It / I Don't Want It:

- I don't need to make this change because......
- Instead of changing now, I can always just......
- My friends and family don't want this because......
- If I don't do this, my life will be......

Are your thoughts getting clearer? If you:

- Want it and need it, you'll put all your effort into achieving it.
- Want it but don't need it, you may expend less effort.
- Need it but don't want it, you may expend some effort.
- Don't want or need it, it's unlikely you'll expend any effort achieving it.

Look at the Steps to Success graphic below. On a scale of 1 to 10, select the number that best describes how you feel about accomplishing your goal.

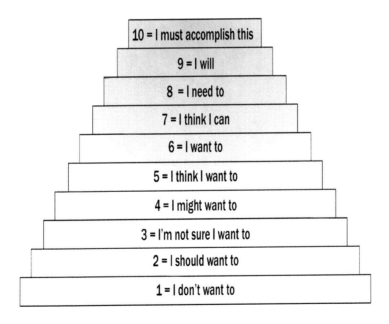

Steps to Success

Have Your Feelings Changed?

Sometimes it helps to gauge where your motivation level is by seeing how your feelings have changed over time.

Rank your answers to the following questions on a scale of 1 – 10 with:

1 = not interested at all

5 = somewhat interested and committed

10 = extremely committed

- How did I feel about achieving this goal five years ago? _____
- How did I feel about achieving this goal a year ago? _____
- How did I feel about achieving this goal a few months ago? _____
- How do I feel about achieving this goal today? _____

At this point, you should have a good idea about what's really motivating you to achieve your goal. Where do you fit in the Need Want Model of Motivation, and what did you learn about your *need to succeed* by completing the questions in each section? Where did you rank yourself on the Steps to Success scale and what's moving you up the ladder? How have your feelings about achieving your goals changed over time and what will make your determination even stronger? When you've completed these exercises, tuck your notes away and refer to them often as you move along. Periodically comparing where you have been to where you are in your change process can be one of the best energizers of all.

Competing Agendas

"The pure and simple truth
is rarely pure and never simple."
~ Author unknown

I'VE ALWAYS SAID that I'd love to be thin – not model thin – but trim, sleek – runner thin. Well, apparently that's not really true. As the years go by, I'm faced with the reality that I'm getting older and wider! Every time I make noises about getting in fabulous shape, I come up with a few dozen reasons – some excellent, some old and tired—why *now* is just not the right time.

The truth is, I don't want to make the sacrifices it would take to have a svelte body. I let my competing agendas, which pit exercising against: the joy of good food, the luxury of reading, watching TV, chatting with friends or listening to music win out. It's a hard truth, but it's *my* truth. I simply have too many competing agendas to make this particular dream come true. Having come to terms with this truth is both liberating and a little sobering. Are you ready for your truth about the change you say you want to make?

Here's a series of questions designed to unearth your competing agendas. Hold your change goal in mind and ask yourself the following questions. Be honest—come clean. This is the time for the naked truth that will expose where you are in the whole change process. It can be powerful to enlist the help of a friend who can work candidly with you in this exercise.

1. ***What is the issue, situation, habit or behavior I want to change?*** Your goal description goes here. Be as clear and specific as you can.

2. ***What have I done in the past to try and change this?*** List any and all efforts you've made – whether complete disasters, partial successes or ongoing attempts. Include the people you talked to about it, the times you cried, fantasized or joked with others about it, classes you've taken, support groups you've attended, books you've read or documentaries you've watched.

3. ***What was the result of each of my efforts?*** Be specific. Did you make new friends, learn something, or get to blame someone?

4. ***How did I feel about the results?*** List each of them separately.

5. ***How did I benefit from each of these results?*** Be honest. If you got sympathy from others about the problem or if your problem was the centre of attention with your family, which allowed you special privileges, then that's at least a temporary benefit, even if the end result was disappointing. You may have also received benefits such as buying new clothes, meeting new people, or learning something new.

6. ***What will my life be like if I no longer get any of these benefits?*** How will you feel without engaging in the activities above.

7. ***Am I really ready to give up these benefits? Really?***

Look carefully at your answers. What did you discover? If you can come through this analysis and feel strongly committed, you're ready to make that change.

Factors that Influence How You Make Change

There are many dynamics at play that influence how people approach and succeed at making changes. Some of the most significant include gender, social cohort, family of origin models and life experiences. Being aware of how these influences play out during the process of setting goals, choosing motivators and developing your change plan, will allow you to capitalize on your strengths and understand your limitations as you move along in the change process. Let's take a look at the components of your perspective, and examine how they've shaped your current approach to change.

The Gender Gap

Often, boys and men tend to be more adventurous than girls and women, in their approach to challenging change. Of course there are exceptions to every rule, and I've certainly met little girls and grown women who were fearless in their pursuit of a goal, but generally speaking, men tend to be bolder and more comfortable with risk and exposure, at least in the beginning.

An example of this is played out before us each week in the currently popular reality series called *Fear Factor.* In it, men and women are pitted against each other in extreme circumstances. Although some women have won the weekly competition, often it's the men who win when extreme risk taking is required. Men are often a little more comfortable with risk, while women often choose a steady calculated approach. How has your gender shaped your current change effort? Do you think it's helping or hindering you? How can you mediate the influence of your gender on your change efforts?

Social Cohort

Your social cohort—the social group with whom you share age and experience—often influences how you approach change. For example the Boomers, those born between 1943 and 1960, represent a social cohort. Growing up in the 1960's has given the Boomers a distinctly different way of seeing themselves and their world from that of their parents' generation. Being the first generation post the Second World War, contributed to their being comfortable with change. Boomers wanted to change the world! They rallied, burned bras, marched in the streets, created and listened to a new type of music, broke racial and cultural barriers and generally wreaked havoc with the status quo.

The events that a social group experiences early in life can stay with them and can influence how they approach change in adulthood. For example, the threat of nuclear war so persistent through the 1950s and 1960s, radically affected how Boomers saw themselves, their personal safety and the world, and consequently has affected how they approach change.

Growing up in southern California, I vividly remember taking part in 'bomb drills'. They would begin with the teacher announcing that someone, somewhere, had dropped a bomb, and that we were to protect ourselves. The teacher would bark out instructions, "Crouch under your desk, put your arms over your heads. Don't look at the light. Wait for the danger to pass." Imagine! It's quite incredible to think of it now. That scene is ludicrous for so many reasons. Those Friday afternoon drills, however, dramatically shaped how I thought about my world.

Surviving has given those of us who are Boomers a sense of invincibility, and yet being continually faced with potential annihilation, has left many with a profound sense of vulnerability. How Boomers have made sense of these, and other experiences, has shaped us as individuals and has also shaped our nation's foreign policy, sexual practices, our experimentation with family forms and our definition of success. Can you identify the events that have happened to your social group that may be influencing how you're approaching this change effort?

Family Modeling

Aside from personality, there's no greater influence on our readiness and willingness to make change than the modeling we saw in our parents, teachers, church members and neighbors. All families go through change – some more dramatic than others. We watched mom and dad change, or not, and decided what should be done. It seems that people either adopt their parents' example of when and how to make changes, or choose to do just the opposite. Often when mom and dad are adventurous, always on the move, looking for the next opportunity, the children grow up feeling comfortable about making change. They see parents who embrace new things, and they get swept into the fun and excitement of the new house, neighborhood, school and activities. When parents have tough experiences with risk and change, their children may develop negative or apprehensive feelings about change as well.

Life Experiences

Under what circumstances have you tried to make changes in the past? What happened?

Paul, a long time brick-layer wanted to start his own construction company. So he developed a business plan and headed off to the bank. His banker told him the economy was soft and that he'd better keep his job for a few years before venturing out on his own. When he told his family of his plans, his father, an old-world family man in his 60s, simply said, "Be happy you have a good paying job. You shouldn't risk your family's future with your crazy dreams."

Sitting back and waiting for the economy to improve didn't feel right to Paul, so against the advice of his banker and family, he bought some used equipment and began to solicit renovation jobs. At first the jobs were small, barely paying for his material costs and labor. However, over time, he began to attract the attention of the construction industry and won some larger contracts. In the first year he netted just enough to feed his family and buy a bit of equipment, but over the course of the following five years, Paul's business grew steadily. Despite the well-intentioned warnings of those around him, he turned his dreams into a successful reality. His success gave him the confidence to take on very large projects, even when he couldn't see exactly how they would work out.

Now, contrast Paul's story with Christine's.

I met Christine at an improvisational class. After completing

111

two years of theatre, she was taking one last class before heading off to Los Angeles to become a television actor. She had quit her job as a lifeguard at the city pool—a job she'd had since high school—sold her possessions, secured an agent and chosen her departure date.

I heard from Christine about two years later when she returned to her home town, disappointed and broke. She had underestimated the time and tenacity it would take to break into the business, and she had run out of money in the pursuit of her dream. It was heartbreaking to see how discouraged she was from not reaching her objective. It was also distressing to see her so defeated by this experience. She labeled herself a failure and vowed never to try anything like that again. She concluded that she was incapable of being anything more than a lifeguard.

Whether it's gender, social cohort, family modeling or life experiences—they all powerfully impact the way we see our ability and the opportunity to change our lives and achieve more success. It's your choice what you learn from these powerful influencers.

Work With Your Personality —Not Against it

"We should take care not to make intellect our god; it has, of course, powerful muscles, but no personality."
~ *Albert Einstein*

PERSONALITY IS THE single most powerful influence on how people make change. Each of us has a personal change style. We have a set of thought patterns and responses that act as a mental schema or backdrop against which we play out change choices. Understanding your personal change style can help you to decide what you need in order to be successful during a time of transition. Knowing how you approach change, where your natural personality traits best fit the change process, and what kinds of information, encouragement and direction you need to maximize your efforts, positions you for victory.

Each of us has the ability to flex the way we interact with the world, but everyone has a particular set of responses that they are most comfortable with. In computer terms, it's your default position—that comfortable set of behaviours that you exhibit if you don't *consciously* choose to act in a different way. In fact, when you're forced to use a style over a long period of time that doesn't allow for, or call upon, your strengths and preferences, inefficiency and burnout can be the result. The best advice is to know your strengths and to lean into them.

When I was growing up I lived a few blocks away from twin boys. Barry, the older twin by four minutes, was outgoing, athletic and talkative. He had lots of friends and loved to be the center of attention. On a bad day he could be bossy and insensitive; he always seemed ready to run ahead of the group at the slightest provocation. His younger brother, Brent, was quiet, studious and serious. He excelled academically and preferred to have only a few close friends with whom he spent time talking and working on projects. Brent was the first kid in our elementary school to run full fledged psychology experiments, using classmates as subjects!

Despite the fact that they had the same parents, grew up in the same house, ate primarily the same food, watched the same television shows, went to the same school, and even dressed alike, these boys were very different. Had they not looked identical, one would never have guessed that they were siblings. Today, Barry is a local TV anchorman, working on his second marriage. He lives in a big city and still loves to surround himself with a gang of admirers. He sails competitively and has moved across the country three times in the past ten years because of his job.

Brent, on the other hand, lives in a small community with his two children, his wife of many years, and works as a computer analyst. He enjoys weekly bridge games with a close group of friends who have met regularly for the past 12 years. Barry and Brent—identical roots—different personalities—different destinies.

From the earliest of times, Philosophers and Psychologists have attempted to classify individuals in order to be able to describe and predict behavior. Over the recent decade countless assessment tools have been developed to help people identify and work with their personality to achieve greater career and personal success.

Your personal style is your particular way of thinking and behaving, which in turn shapes your daily life and interactions with others and ultimately determines your future. As second nature as breathing, your personality sets you apart and differentiates you from others. Becoming familiar with your style can provide you with a critical tool in the process of making the changes you want, or responding to the changes someone else is making.

By observing personality, you can see how an individual makes choices, processes information, gravitates towards a profession, manages relationships, chooses hobbies, and particularly, how he or she approaches change. Your natural approach to people and things will shape how you should proceed with any change effort.

Change Style Index

The *Change Style Index* is a self assessment tool designed to assist you in quickly determining your natural change style. As you learn about how you prefer to approach fluid environments, you'll be better able to ask for what you want, cooperate with others and find better ways of working your change plan.

In the lists below there are descriptors. Put a checkmark by the ones that best describe you – most of the time. Don't dwell on them; your first response is the best.

Section 1	Section 2
[__] Competitive	[__] Optimistic
[__] Self starter	[__] Charismatic
[__] Assertive	[__] Outgoing
[__] Inquisitive	[__] Big picture person
[__] Outcome oriented	[__] Friendly
[__] Risk taker	[__] Confident
[__] Bold	[__] Verbal
[__] Independent	[__] Likes variety
[__] Easily bored	[__] Strong communicator
[__] Decisive	[__] Not detail oriented

Section 3

[__] Methodical
[__] Empathic
[__] Dependable
[__] Systematic
[__] Patient
[__] Objective
[__] Good listener
[__] Steady
[__] Persistent
[__] Mentor

Section 4

[__] Disciplined
[__] Cautious
[__] Loyal
[__] Private
[__] High standards
[__] Accurate
[__] Logical
[__] Compliant
[__] Careful
[__] Organized

Tally the checks in each section and record the totals below. Most people will have more check marks in one section than the others. Although the scores may be close, you'll find that your style is more accurately described by one, or perhaps two, of the groups of descriptors.

Section 1 _____   Section 3 _____

Section 2 _____   Section 4 _____

Changers Come In All Styles

Section 1
The Alpha Changer

Alpha Changers like to lead the pack. They're big picture thinkers and prefer to be included at the beginning of a project. They're goal oriented risk takers who love a challenge. Alpha Changers like to be in control and are often seen by others as leaders.

Change Assets
Focused on results
Creative visionary
Quick thinker
Competitive

Others: _____

Change Liabilities
Impatient with others
Bored with too much detail
Controlling
Driving

Others: _____

Section 2
The Persuasive Changer

Persuasive Changers love center stage! They're animated, energetic and like to find the fun in every situation. They're strong communicators and can use their considerable talent to persuade just about anyone who will listen. They're curious, impulsive and can sometimes lack the stamina to see a project or plan through to the end.

Change Assets

Likes to talk over plans
Demonstrates enthusiasm
Good at persuading others
Strong communicator

Others: _____

Change Liabilities

Makes hasty decisions
Doesn't pay attention to details
Flamboyant / excitable
May not see problems ahead

Others: _____

Section 3
The Supportive Changer

Everyone loves the Supportive Changer. They're the team's champion, always concerned with how the change will affect others. They're patient and thorough, which makes them valuable resources for content and expertise. They have a way with people and are generally trusted and sought out as advisors and mentors.

Change Assets	Change Liabilities
Cares how the group feels	Can appear unmotivated
Likes to share experiences	May be a "people pleaser"
Recognizes roadblocks early	Too cautious
Persists at achieving the goal	Resists sudden changes
Others: _____	Others: _____

Section 4
The Intentional Changer

Intentional Changers like to plan for change and take a systematic approach to achieving a goal. They're methodical and they like lots of information. They're often uncomfortable leading change, but are extremely adept in the assessment and evaluation phases of a change effort. Their strong sense of loyalty, attention to detail and quality will shine through when required to stay the course to achieve the desired results.

Change Assets	Change Liabilities
Factually confident	Tend to be perfectionists
Like structure	Change resistant
Thinks things through	Worries and may procrastinate
Able to be objective	Tends to be critical
Others: _____	Others: _____

When you have determined your change style, read through the next chapter to see how your natural preferences can help or challenge your plans for change.

Capitalizing on Assets—
Limiting Liabilities

"The ability to flex your style to
collaborate with another
is directly related to the height
of your self esteem."
~ Peggy Grall

ALL CHANGE TAKES place in an environment rich with other people's styles. Most change efforts will require you to work closely with family, friends, co-workers, professionals and others. The more you know about what others need from you that's different than what you need, the better you'll be able to give and receive help, ideas, information and support.

Reflect on the style descriptions in this section. Think about the people who are close to you. Try to guess the style of your partner, children, best friend and co-workers. Is your boss an Alpha or an Intentional? Is your fitness trainer a Supporter? Are your children Persuaders? How do they see the world? What do they need? How can you work with them to create the synergy you need to move your change effort forward? Here are a few ideas to get you started, but try to come up with more that refine and accurately reflect those in your circle of influence.

Alpha Changers need you to:

- get to the point—they don't need or want much detail,
- brainstorm and mind map with them to capture their ideas,

119

- accept that they like to be in control, but they appreciate your direct input,
- give them public credit for their ideas and efforts,
- help them see the 'right now' issues as they tend to be future oriented,
- encourage them to pay attention to work/life balance,
- let them know when they're moving too fast for you,
- feed them knowledge – they love to learn,
- let them know when they haven't heard all you've said.

To collaborate with the Alphas in my life, I need to...

Persuasive Changers need you to:

- help them follow through on projects and deadlines —they can easily get distracted,
- make projects and tasks fun,
- acknowledge them publicly – they'll do the same for you,
- let them talk out difficult issues,
- clarify your expectations – set time lines, due dates,
- prevent them from dominating the conversation,
- use their persuasive talents effectively,
- take them seriously—they can appear frivolous at times,
- give them important, but brief assignments.

To collaborate with the Persuasive Changers in my life, I need to...

Supportive Changers need you to:

- recognize and utilize their considerable expertise,
- put them in charge of the *people* issues,
- allow them to tackle difficult projects one piece at a time,

- allow them to grapple with a new idea in small group discussions and hands on activities,
- allow them time to make a decision—they can easily see both sides,
- keep surprises to a minimum,
- give them negative feedback privately and respectfully,
- explain requirements in practical, concrete examples,
- help them put action steps to their vision and goals.

To collaborate with the Supportive Changers in my life, I need to…

Intentional Changers need you to:

- give them time to gather all the information that they will need to act,
- supply them with the facts that they need to make a sound decision – use graphs and charts and allow time for detailed Q &A,
- honor their past achievements – this allows them to move with the new initiatives,
- maintain as much structure as possible during the change,
- help them see the big picture—they can get lost in the details,
- remember that they're taking in the information you give out – make it real,
- remind them of the relationship issues in any situation,
- lean on them for the critical follow-through, so important to long-term projects,
- see them for the accurate experts that they are.

To collaborate with the Intentional Changers in my life, I need to…

Extroverts and Introverts

It appears that we are born with a particular temperament; a natural, almost physical preference for interacting with the world around us. Although there are several ways to understand and describe temperament, I commonly think of the two broad categories of Extroversion and Introversion. Extroversion is, simply put, when a person prefers to draw energy from the outside world of people, activities and things. In contrast, Introverts prefer to draw their energy from their internal world of ideas, emotions and impressions. Temperament appears to be the one thing about us that is relatively fixed. Although we can take on the behaviors of the opposite temperament for a period of time, most people feel drained and out of sorts when they step, or are pushed too far out of their natural comfort zone.

Alphas and Persuaders tend to be extroverted, although there are certainly people in this personality style that prefer a more reserved approach to life. Consider the following if you're an Extroverted Alpha or a Persuader.

Extroverts will be inspired to change more easily if they:

- make the change entertaining.
- talk to friends, get a change buddy, join a support group.
- get a mentor or coach,
- interview people who have achieved what they desire,
- preview the change,
- challenging themselves in the risk stage.
- dream, wish, hope, fantasize how the change will effect them directly.
- stay focused on the possibilities.
- stick with what *seems* right.
- picture success—meditation, prayer, visualization.
- look for a unique approach to the change—alternative educational routes, new fitness routines, unusual career paths, etc.

Some considerations for Extroverts:

- don't mistake activity for results.
- consider carefully the viability of your goals.
- take your time.
- learn to depend on others.
- get the facts—before jumping in.
- determine how the change will affect others.
- be realistic with yourself and others.
- carefully consider and evaluate the costs before beginning.
- put emotions aside—determine if the change is practical.
- get information about methods, probable outcomes.
- design a solid plan and stick to it.
- get a step-by step approach mapped out before beginning.
- finish what you start!

Intentional and Supportive Changers tend to be more Introverted. Consider the following if you are an Introverted Intentional or Supportive Changer:

Introverts will be inspired to change more easily if they:

- develop a detailed plan for change,
- gather the facts—read about other successful people.
- get a one-on-one coach or mentor.
- find a good method for pushing themselves into action,
- break the task into doable steps.
- choose one thing at a time.
- find models, methods, formulas that fit what they're trying to do.
- set a goal—then stretch it.
- make sure this change fits with their values and the rest of their life.
- make their plan concrete—get the facts, the timelines, and the necessary tools.

Some considerations for Introverts:

- set a limit on how long you'll research the change before taking action.

- don't' fall prey to *paralysis by analysis*.

- get an objective opinion of probabilities.

- use proven methods.

- use charts, journals, concrete rewards to chart progress.

- select practical pay-offs for milestones in the process.

- choose enticing rewards for yourself.

- question if this change is for you.

- choose goals that fit your value system.

- look for alternative ways to accomplish a task.

- visualize the possible.

- don't limit yourself/others.

- believe in your capacity to change.

- look for ways to have fun with this—it doesn't all have to be work.

- be flexible—look for the need to modify your plan along the way.

- look for synergy opportunities—other people can add a lot to your success.

For every rule there's an exception. If you're more of an Extrovert, you may still want to consider some of the suggestions for Introverts. The same holds true for Introverts. We're complex creatures. Holding too rigidly to labels can box us in. Consider the ideas in this chapter and make your personality work for you.

Going Public

*"A lie gets half way around the world
before the truth gets its pants on."*
~ Winston Churchill

WHEN YOU'RE PLANNING a change, especially a big one, a key consideration is deciding whom you should or should not tell. Going public is a very individual decision and there are no hard and fast rules. For some, going public is the best decision. For others, it can be ill-advised, or even dangerous, to tell certain people about your plans.

After 15 unhappy years of marriage, Maggie was making plans to leave her abusive husband. She had tried to leave before, only to have her husband find out and retaliate with increased anger and abuse. This time she kept her plans between herself and her therapist. The only other person who knew she was leaving was her best friend Liz.

Maggie chose a date and began to put money away, secured a place to stay and systematically made copies of all of her important personal documents. She contacted a lawyer to ask about a number of legal issues, and the day before her planned departure, she alerted the school where her children attended.

The day came and after her husband left for work she got her children off to school, and called her best friend who had a pick-up truck waiting. The two women loaded her and her children's personal belongings, and enough food for a few days, onto the truck. Maggie wrote a brief and blunt letter to her husband, and then left. She stayed temporarily at Liz's house and alerted the police of her move and her fear of retaliation. Maggie's private and careful planning was her ticket out of a very dangerous situation for herself and her children.

Contrast Maggie's story with the experience of a client I was coaching who decided he wanted to retire early. *Dean went public in a big way with his plans to make a change. He began his change plan by talking it over at length with his wife, best friend, financial advisor, pastor and supervisor. He consulted me, his doctor, a real estate broker, the company's Human Resources benefits person and a few retirement communities before he ever took a step. Virtually everyone in Dean's world knew he was planning early retirement.*

By going public he accumulated a tremendous amount of valuable information and support that helped him make the transition, and he was able to benefit from the expertise of others. As a result, he decided to put off retiring for one year longer, for a number of financial reasons. At the end of the year his wife was able to ease out of her position and negotiate an excellent early retirement package as well. Throughout his final year at work, his friends and family shared several great ideas with him about hobbies, alternative work situations, economical vacation spots and valuable organizations to join. All this, because he told everyone in his world that he was considering making a change.

Who needs to know what you're going through? When do they need to know? Sharing your plans for change, or not, is your choice. If you decide to go public—you will need to decide who needs to know, and when it is best to tell them.

Change Buddies

"There was a definite process by which one made people into friends, and it involved talking to them and listening to them for hours at a time."
~ *Rebecca West*

IF YOU'VE EVER tried to make a change without the right support, you know how difficult that can be. A key element of successful change for many people comes in the form of a change buddy—a friend who's in your corner all the way. Better yet, someone who's on the same path.

When you're making changes that affect others, you can often enlist their support in helping you stay on track. For example, if you're considering changing jobs, your change buddy may be able to help you by: role-playing how you can approach your boss, editing your letter of resignation, helping you prepare for an interview or consider a new job offer. Involving others in your plans can also lend a degree of urgency to accomplishing your tasks. When you want to quit, a supportive nudge by your change buddy can get you back in the game.

If, on the other hand, those who will be affected by your plans don't want you to succeed, it can be best to seek alternative support to fill the role. Those people who don't want you to change your relationship with them, your body, or anything else about yourself, are *not* the people you want to count on for encouragement and support on your journey.

Helen and Stacy had been best friends since high school. Their lifestyle choices had been very different, but they'd always enjoyed each other's company. Helen felt strongly about raising her children herself, so she chose to be a stay-at-home mom and contribute to the family income by doing part time work. Stacy had two active children and chose to pursue a full time career in retail. When Helen decided she wanted to start her own catering company, she made her first call to Stacy.

Helen wanted to make sweet boxes for corporate gift giving. She consulted Stacy to gather information about the corporate market, and Stacy enthusiastically offered her advice based on her experience. Stacy helped Helen with merchandizing ideas and she acted as Helen's cheerleader every step of the way.

When Helen's youngest daughter got the chicken pox, right in the middle of delivery deadlines, Stacy was there to babysit her. When Helen's husband began complaining about the constant mess in the kitchen, it was Stacy who encouraged her to stay on track. It was Stacy who 'ooohed' and 'aaahed' over the baskets when they were finally ready for delivery. And it was Stacy who sent Helen a 'you go, girl' card for her tenacity and clarity of vision.

Today, Helen has a thriving catering business that specializes in corporate goody baskets, thank you cards and gifts. Helen has told me many times that if it hadn't been for Stacy, she would not have had the courage to transform her dream into reality.

The support of a good friend can be a powerful tool to help you keep on going when the going gets rough. There may be people just itching to support you—people that would love to see you make this change and who would relish being part of your success. Do you need a change buddy? If so, who should it be?

Simplify Your Life

*"Be steady and well ordered in your life so that
you can be fierce and original in your work."*
~ *Gustave Flaubert*

LONG DISTANCE RUNNERS know that in order to run their best race, they have to shed anything that has the potential of bogging them down. Serious competitors even shave body hair for the sake of aerodynamics. Determined changers are similar to champion runners; they discard and/or gain mastery over things and relationships that threaten to impede their progress. Being free of excess baggage, both tangible and psychological, will allow you to see the path ahead more clearly, move more quickly and switch directions with greater ease and agility. Consider the following ways to purge dead weight from your home, routines and self.

Get organized

Knowing where to find what you need, when you need it, is foundational to making successful change. Before beginning a change effort, thoroughly clean out your garage, car, closets, basement, kitchen and work files. Categorize and systematize your bills, telephone numbers, wills and insurance policies. Secure a reliable back-up system for your computer. In other words, before beginning a change effort, put your life in order.

Get rid of unnecessary 'Stuff'

The more you're attached to your *stuff,* the more difficult it will be if you have to give up some of your *stuff* in order to grab hold of something new. The average North American, middle class home could outfit another home of equal size without buying anything new. Most people could sell, give to a consignment shop, donate, or simply give away clothes, old furniture, used toys, old books, unused novelty items or old appliances and never miss them. If you're going to stride easily and confidently into the next phase of your life, you may need to unload some of your *stuff.*

It doesn't really matter how much *stuff* you have. But you need to ask yourself if your *stuff,* and the time it takes to care for it, or your attachment to it, is preventing you from doing what you need to do.

Are you so attached to your adult toys that you can't leave your well-paying job, even though it's compromising your health and interfering with the family life you really want?

Are you putting yourself and your children at risk by staying in an abusive relationship because, by staying, you get to live in a great house?

Fix it—or throw it out

A squeaky door hinge, a leaky faucet, a car that won't start, appliances that need repair, burnt out light bulbs, slippery walkways, and slow clocks—fix them, replace them or throw them away. Being distracted by the annoyance of broken, faulty things will slow your change process.

Learn to delegate

To the degree that you can afford to, delegate those chores and responsibilities that you don't like or don't do well. Hire help when you can, and barter for services when you can't afford to pay. Case in point:

When I was single-parenting in Yellowknife, the capital city of the Northwest Territories in Canada, one of the tasks I dreaded most was piling three small kids into a frozen vehicle on cold, winter mornings. In the winter months it was routinely -20° to - 40° and starting a car in that kind of weather was brutal for this California-born girl. I had a neighbor who didn't have a car. So we made a deal that worked very well for both of us. In exchange for a ride to work, he would come over early, start the car, scrape the windows and help me buckle the kids in. The beauty of our arrangement still warms my heart. We both got exactly what we needed and no money exchanged hands.

Be creative! What do you do or have that someone else could make use of, and who has what you need?

Get out of negative relationships

There are people in this world that you just don't want or need in your life. They can suck the life out of you, take your time and energy and leave you feeling totally and utterly drained. They may be your neighbors, friends, committee members, co-workers or in-laws. Commit today to ease out of the negative relationships that are draining you of the energy you need for your change effort. Maybe the change you want to make, and the reason you bought this book, was to learn to disentangle yourself from negative people.

Start first with those easiest to exclude from your life. Perhaps it's your paper carrier, hairdresser or dry cleaner that's sharing their negativity with you. Eliminate contact with them immediately. For most people this should be fairly easy since we generally only have superficial contact with these types of service providers. As you learn the skill of terminating negative relationships and begin to feel the difference it makes in your energy level and outlook, you'll be more resolved to make the break from more significant relationships.

Learn to block interruptions

You don't owe anyone your time. Purchase and use a phone answering machine, and screen your calls. Install a peep hole in your front door. Look before you open your door. This not only makes good security sense, but you can also choose to whom you will and will not respond. Put a *No Soliciting* sign near your front door. Most door to door purchasing is risky at best, so why waste your time listening to pitches from people you don't know about products you don't need. Spend that time on yourself and your family.

Manage your time well

The average adult watches an inordinate number of hours of TV per year. If you're engaged in a serious change effort, use that time for reading books that can provide you with good ideas, inspiration or sharpen your skills. Great documentaries and *How To* videos abound on the issue you're trying to change—rent them, watch them and nourish your spirit. Immerse yourself in good writing. Read wisdom literature that contains the secrets of living a meaningful life.

I've always loved the following story. It speaks to the power of small changes.

The Trash Lady

The story is told of an old woman in the heart of Anywhere, U.S.A., who lived alone in her home surrounded only by her 'stuff'—the junk of life—the trash of her past. Exaggerated stories circled the neighborhood about her unusual habit of collecting garbage until all the young children in the area were completely terrified of going anywhere near her house because of its eerie mystery.

One day, in a gesture of kindness and self-imposed bravery, a young boy cautiously ventured toward her house, knocked on her door and offered her a small bouquet of flowers. Living up to her reputation, the old woman accepted them with a grunt and quickly slammed the door shut. Not knowing exactly where to put the little boy's gift, she decided to temporarily place the flowers in her living room. But when she looked for a spot, all she saw were old magazines, dirty dishes, empty boxes piled sky-high, overflowing ash trays and clothes strewn all over the furniture. In an uncharacteristic move she grabbed a dust cloth and cleared a place on an end table and set the flowers down.

The woman admired the flowers, but soon felt that the flowers and the end table stood out in stark contrast to the rest of the room. So she cleared off the other end table. She stepped back and surveyed the room. She liked the clean orderliness of the end tables so much that she soon cleared all the junk from the coffee table. As each piece of furniture became visible, she began to see how dark and cluttered the rest of the room looked. She set about to straighten first the clothes and then the old magazines. Her efforts were infectious and soon the entire room was restored to order.

After cleaning the living room, she moved on to other rooms. When she had transformed her entire house, she began to venture out into her yard. "A beautiful house should have a beautiful yard," she said aloud. As she began spending more time outside, the children in the neighborhood started coming into her yard, hesitant at first and then in droves. She began baking cookies and welcoming the children into her yard. She was no longer the trash lady, but the kind lady on the corner with the pretty yard—proof positive big changes often start with small gestures. Start today to get the stuff of your life in order. Sort it, clean it, fix it and organize it. You won't be ready for the *new* until the old is in order. Simplify one area of your life at a time—and watch the miracles happen!

Assert Yourself

"You don't always win when you stand up
for yourself—but you never win if you don't."
~ *Ellen Bravo*

WHEN INVOLVED IN a major change, you can approach the process, and everyone involved in it, in one of three ways. You can either be Aggressive, Passive or Assertive.

The *Aggressive* Approach

To interact with someone aggressively is to operate on the assumption that *I count—You don't*. That is, whatever you think, feel, need or want is more important than the other person's needs. An aggressive approach is accompanied by a lack of mutual respect, very little active listening and a conversation style that is often peppered with veiled threats and criticism. An aggressive stance invites an atmosphere of winning and losing. An example of aggressive change behavior may be when you only take yourself into consideration in the change process. While change choices are often not popular with everyone in your life, you should approach the change with understanding and compassion for those who will be impacted by your choices.

The *Passive* Approach

To handle life or relationships in a passive manner is to abdicate your ideas, feelings or needs in favor of another's. This position operates on the, *You count—I don't* premise. What *you* think, feel, require or desire are given up to accommodate another's needs. You either don't offer yourself in the interaction, or you allow the other person, group or colleague to keep you from participating in conversations, decisions and behaviors that have the potential for self expression.

Often passive people employ covert methods to get their voice heard and their needs met. Not sharing one's ideas or maintaining the status quo may seem like a good idea at first, but a position of non-participation comes back to haunt most people.

An example of a passive change position would be telling yourself that you can't really make a difference in your life. You think that you have to wait for someone else to change and hope that you'll like their choice. Passivity is *doormat* behavior.

CALLING ALL APPROVAL JUNKIES
AND DOORMATS

Many of us were taught as children to try to *please all the people all the time* – or as close as we could get to it. Many of us are still doing it. Are you? Have you bought into the cycle of denying yourself to get the approval of others? How is that working for you?

Many adults are continually searching for ways to make people *happy*, hoping for approval in return. This is a life formula for self-deprivation and a recipe that always creates resentment and a loss of dignity. Being dependent on approval for self-esteem—so dependant that we barter away all our time, energy and personal preferences to get it, ruins the very sweetness of being alive. It separates us from our true selves, prevents true intimacy with others and turns us into cauldrons of concealed rage. Not a pretty picture. If you're an approval junkie or a doormat—stop it!

There is another position that can be taken; a variation on the passivity theme called Passive Aggressive. When you behave passively it doesn't feel very good. When you consciously, or un-knowingly, put yourself in a one-down position to others, adopting a *You count—I don't* stance, resentment inevitably builds. If you do this long enough and/or with enough people you will find yourself gravitating towards ways to even the score; you will *make yourself count*—at all costs. And the costs are often high. At the office, passive aggression can take the form of gossip or back-stabbing; the passive aggressive person takes revenge on those they perceive to have slighted them or left them out. In personal relationships people will withdraw love and affection, covertly or overtly demonstrating the pain of not being important in their own eyes. Don't take this path. No one wins. You count in life and in your relationships, so step up, speak out, and contribute your ideas, energy and perspective to the conversations and activities you are part of. Be up-front with what you need and want, or you will be tempted to find less attractive ways to feel worthy.

The *Assertiveness* Approach

The only healthy approach to events and other people is to employ an, *I count—You count* philosophy. High on respect and inclusion, this view translates into an open sharing of ideas, an elevated level of trust and an environment where both parties can effectively face, discuss and resolve whatever comes up.

Assertive people speak clearly, listen carefully, and acknowledge the contributions of themselves and others. They value relationships over outcomes and work hard to reach win-win solutions. In an intense change program, assertive people can be counted on to speak up, speak out and hold in high regard the voices of those around them. They use 'I' language—speaking for themselves and allowing others to do the same. Assertive changers accept that others have the right to choose their own behavior in a situation. They respect the reactions of others and maintain a high level of respect for themselves and others throughout the change process.

Think carefully about which of the three approaches described here is the one you use most often. I suggest that you adopt an assertive approach as often as you possibly can as you move forward.

Stay Informed

"You think you understand the situation,
but what you don't understand is
that the situation just changed."
~ *Putnam Investments*

VITAL INFORMATION OFTEN comes at lightening speed in a transition. People often stop listening once the initial announcement has been made, the bad-news letter has been read or the initial trauma weathered, the very time to be listening more intently. What you need to know most when you are changing, may just come from unexpected sources. If you are responding to the choices someone else has initiated, once you catch your breath, start looking for the information *you* will need to get going.

In preparation for this *big, fat change*, you may need to: assess your financial status, get a physical from a health professional, review your will, check your calendar, evaluate the package, gather purchasing information or talk to a real estate broker. Use the web, the library, association trade journals and newsletters, consumer guides, audio and video tutorials, hot lines and word of mouth to find out what you need to know. Write it down – your memory may not be at its best right now.

Information, whether it came to you unsolicited or you searched high and low for it, should translate to increased levels of personal insight. Take what you learn and ask yourself how it applies to you. Not what it means for your mother, spouse, co-worker or best friend—you!

Take a Chance

"Don't forget folks—the less you bet,
the more you lose when you win."
~ From a stickman at a Las Vegas casino

KENNY ROGERS SAID it best, "You got to know when to hold 'em, know when to fold 'em, know when to walk away – and know when to run." Some people try to minimize the stress of a transition by shying away from anything additional in their lives that smacks of being new, different, risky or unfamiliar. When you find yourself thinking that you'd better just lay low and not rock the boat—think again.

> *"The price of self-destiny is never cheap. And in certain circumstances, it's unthinkable. But to achieve the marvelous, it is precisely the unthinkable that must be thought."*
>
> - Author unknown

While playing it safe may be a short term solution to feeling too much discomfort or fear, it's also a short-sighted way of managing the stress of change. When you stop taking calculated risks, you interact with life as a spectator. You may learn something by observing others while they play, but learning curves are flat on the sidelines. Without *game time* you lose your edge. Without the sweat and ache of real time struggling with the issues, you can get out of shape for the next big change that comes along. It's when you are stepping out and grabbing hold of the tough stuff, that you gain the all-important change skills you need.

So, stretch yourself today. You'll be in better shape to meet tomorrow's challenges. Develop a greater tolerance for constant change in your personal game plan. Embrace mid-course corrections and raw surprises. Be willing to feel your way along—to *wing it* when the situation calls for it. Think of your life as having movable parts. Flex to fit the demands of the situation, instead of always trying to make people and events fit your idea of how life is *supposed* to be.

Your ability to change what you want changed will require you to risk some important things – maybe even your reputation. Take risks – not necessarily mind numbing, white-knuckled risks, but those bold steps that have the potential to really make a difference.

Find Support

"I went to a bookstore the other day.
I asked the woman behind the counter
where the self-help section was.
She said, 'If I told you that,
it would defeat the whole purpose.'"
~ Brian Kiley

MOST PEOPLE NEED other people to help them achieve their best. Who will that be for you? Do you need a support group, an exercise buddy, role model, mentor, coach, or cheerleader? There's a distinct difference between making others accountable for your success and enlisting people to help you with specific parts of your program.

You may want to have a number of support resources along the way. In the beginning, you may want to have individuals or groups who can provide guidance, information or point the way. Later on in the difficult phase, you may need more of a cheerleader or coach who can keep you on track and focused if your tendency has been to quit half-way. Towards the end of the process, you may benefit from the services of someone trained in helping you make social adjustments to your new lifestyle.

There are several categories of helping professionals. The following is a brief description of the profile and areas of expertise for each. While time spent with a best friend can be *just what the doctor ordered,* many people benefit from the support of a professional during times of intense transition.

Self Help

Here's a brief look at the various types of help available. Trying various avenues for helping yourself through a difficult time is a very sound strategy. It's inexpensive, confidential and effective. You can do it at home, in the car, while you're on vacation or on breaks at work. Self-helpers use books, tapes, videos and tele-seminars. There's a wealth of information and help available from libraries, issue-specific associations, on-line resources and self-guided programs.

Peer Support

People need people. For centuries men and women have turned to each other for comfort, ideas, support and practical help during challenging times—and for good reason. People help each other through peer led support groups like Alcoholics Anonymous, Separated Anonymous, professional executive networks or cancer survivor groups. These groups are comprised of people who are facing similar health, career or personal challenges. You join, pay a nominal fee and contribute your expertise in exchange for the time and expertise of other members.

Professional Support

Helping professionals can be found offering their expertise in clinics, hospitals, fitness gyms, associations, private practices and boardrooms of large corporations. The first step in finding the right professional is to decide exactly what kind of help you need. Do you want an individual practitioner, or do you need a team of experts? Do you need assistance with personal, family, legal, financial, career, health or a combination of issues? Finding the right peer support and/or professional people to help you can mean the difference between struggling and soaring towards your goal.

Does Therapy Really Help?

*"I know you believe you understood
what you thought I said,
but I am not sure you realize
that what you heard is not what I meant."*
~ Unknown

"DOES THERAPY REALLY work?" Many people have asked me that question, in a variety of ways, over the years. The answer is a resounding yes! In *The Heart and Soul of Change,* which examines 60 years of outcome research on the effectiveness of therapy, M. Hubble, B. Duncan and Scott Miller concluded the following:

"These reviews leave little doubt. Therapy is effective. Treated patients fare much better than the untreated, with 80% of the treated persons being better off than the untreated samples." The study further reports on the sustainability factor of therapy, stating that, *"Psychotherapy is, in general effective, efficient, and lasting."*

What makes therapy so effective? In brief, it appears that it's a combination of four common factors that converge to achieve a successful outcome:

1. the quality of the relationship between therapist and client.

2. the degree of hope the therapist and client share

3. the techniques the therapist uses, and

4. the changes that the client makes on their own, between sessions

The therapeutic relationship, or how good the fit is between the therapist and the client, is a major factor in therapy, contributing a whopping 30% to the likelihood of success.

So what does all of this mean for you? If you think therapy would be helpful to you right now as you're making these changes, go for it! Choose your therapist well. Ask for referrals from friends who have had positive experiences, interview a few therapists and see how you feel about each one before committing. Therapy is never a walk in the park, but you should feel confident that you're being heard and that the therapist you've chosen has the skills to help you. Then get to work!

MD General Practitioners

These professionals are limited in their availability and often don't have the desire to provide counseling for personal issues. They do have the ability to monitor your physical health and write prescriptions for the kinds of medications that you might require to help you through a period of depression, or the anxiety that sometimes follows a sudden loss or tragic event.

MD Specialists

Psychiatrists and general practitioner psychotherapists are often the medical professionals people seek out during times of intense personal transition. Their services are covered by provincial or state health care plans and they have prepared themselves for counseling individuals and families by taking additional training beyond their medical degrees.

Registered Psychologists

A registered psychologist is a person who is academically prepared to do assessments and counseling by obtaining a PhD. in psychology or a related discipline.

Psychologists are regulated by the government and must adhere to a strict code of ethics and practices. Their services are often covered by industry health insurance plans and you'll find them working in clinics, hospitals and private practices. These professionals often specialize in helping a particualar part of the population; some focusing on relationships, family, addictions and other such issues.

Psychotherapists/ Counselors

These professionals have prepared themselves to provide counseling services by obtaining an undergraduate degree in psychology, social work, education or other related fields; they commonly further their training with a master's degree in one of these areas of study. They work in private practices, clinics, hospitals, schools and community agencies. These professionals are often the counselors of choice for Employee Assistance Programs—a counseling service provided at no cost to employees through their employer.

Like a registered psychologist, psychotherapists and counselors often specialize in a particular area of expertise and they too must adhere to their professional association's code of ethics and practices. Their services are increasingly being covered by industry health insurance plans and they often offer a *sliding scale* of payment—a fee for service determined by a client's financial situation.

Social Workers

Social Workers generally hold a bachelor's degree in social work and work in clinics, hospitals, schools, group homes and community agencies. They aren't generally formally trained in psychotherapy techniques, but act in a supportive role in many agencies, clinics and community programs.

Alternative Therapies

The list of alternative helpers and their approaches to helping could fill the rest of this book. There are spiritual helpers such as pastors, priests and rabbis. There are complementary physical helpers such as chiropractors, naturopaths and Reiki healers. And the list goes on.

Is professional help right for you?

So when do you need to go to a therapist or counselor?

Here's an easy way of assessing the answer:

- Do you want to fast track this change process?
- Do you find it helpful to *talk out* your feelings and ideas?
- Have you been unsuccessful with this change process in the past?
- Are there personal considerations about this change that you would prefer to deal with in private?
- Could you use a sounding board through this transition that's free of the natural bias and vested interests of family and friends?

If the answer to any or all of these questions is *yes,* then you would probably benefit from the assistance that a professional can provide. If not, then continue with your current support system and re-consider professional help at another point in the process.

If cost is a factor, and it often is for people in transition, ask the professional if he/she has a sliding scale—a fee schedule that accommodates a client's financial status. Often people in private practice have more latitude in making concessions on fees than those working in government, health care institutions or large corporations.

There are no hard and fast rules about seeking support or professional help. Choose the best route for you. You can always see a professional for a while, take a break and then resume your sessions when you feel the need. Reputable therapists will allow you the flexibility to choose when you want to access their services.

As you know, I've been a therapist for years. As long as you want or need my encouragement and help, I will be within the pages of this book—accessible at any time.

Get Set
Review

*"Try not to become a man of success
but rather try to become a man of value."*
~ *Albert Einstein*

GOOD FOR YOU, you've completed another section! By now, you're probably feeling revved up and ready to move on to the next phase of your transformation. But before you do, take a few minutes to check your progress. Skim over the list below and review each item to see if you've done all the work involved in examining each idea.

- Are you prepared to trust the process?

- Do you understand the Cycle of Change and the Cycle of Grief and Loss and how to help yourself through each step?

- Have you identified and documented your motivators?

- Are you aware of, and compensating for, your competing agendas ?

- Do you understand what is influencing how you navigate change?

- Did you complete the Change Style Index?

- Do you need to go public yet? Ever?

- Have you enlisted a change buddy?

- Have you eliminated the *unnecessary* from your life yet?

- Are you being assertive with yourself and others?

- Do you have ways to keep yourself and others informed along the way?

- Have you decided which risks make sense to take?

- Will you need to find professional support? If so, have you?

GO!

Dark Alleys
and Danger Zones

"Feel the fear and do it anyway."
~ Susan Jeffers

THERE WILL BE some dark and dangerous places on the road to discovering your new self; some places where it's best not to dwell—heck, it's best not even to go there in the first place! In this section I'm going to point them out to you and then suggest methods for handling yourself when faced with the trials and temptations of each one.

Steep Learning Curves

When we humans are learning—we're tense! Learning new ways of thinking and responding can create anxiety, and when you're making significant changes, you'll be learning rapidly. Think about when you were first learning to drive a car. How did you feel when you first got behind the wheel? If you were like most people, you were probably stiff necked, jerky, overly cautious, and constantly trying to anticipate your next move. You were learning and you weren't sure what to do next. You had to both drive the car and mentally translate the vehicle code into real driving— all at the same time—and it was stressful!

Take heart. Nothing is wrong. This is a normal response to change. Even if you asked for this change, you'll feel shaky at first. Accept that you'll be unsure and uptight some of the time. Don't expect too much of yourself too soon. Forgive your mistakes and keep going.

Sidetracked?

Intention alone is not enough to make significant and lasting change. It's easy to lose momentum and convince yourself that something more important or more urgent needs your attention.

The truly committed changers are doggedly determined to find the right path and stay on it. They find the tools they need and then plow their way towards losing weight, quitting bad habits, becoming more assertive, learning to share themselves, or whatever they've committed to changing. For these change champions, the *how* is there and the *way* is doable, and they don't let anything or anyone sidetrack their efforts.

Discouraged?

It's common, even for the most ardent changer, to become discouraged. Has that happened to you in the past? Have you started down the path towards your goal, only to let slow progress or the resistance of others bring you to a halt?

Have you stopped monitoring your progress, working your plan, reviewing the essentials, or utilizing your support system? Determine now to finish the course! When you find yourself getting sidetracked—stop! Regroup and refocus. Pick a time to begin again—a new start date should never be more than two days in the future.

When I was growing up my little sister and I fought over pretty much everything. We were four years apart and were always doing battle to get our parents' attention, dominate more space in the bedroom or to confiscate "stuff" from each other.

But mostly we fought about ... who was right! It didn't seem to matter what the issue was, we saw just about everything differently. We'd start out calmly talking about something—boys, clothes, our parents, but somehow those discussions always ended in a screaming match. It wasn't long before we'd be yelling at each other. I'd insist she see it my way, and she'd refuse to concede. I didn't have very sophisticated conflict resolution skills in those days, so I'd hold her arms behind her back in a rather uncomfortable position and repeat over and over, "Give up. Say I'm right. Say it. Say it. Say I'm right." She would wail and scream and I'd tighten my grip until she finally screeched, "Uncle." Crying 'uncle' meant that I'd won. She'd given in. She'd put up a valiant effort, but my size and determination had beaten her down.

Many times my sister gave up just when she was about to win. I could only maintain my hold on her for so long, and if she'd have hung in a bit longer, she would have been free.

Do you ever feel like this thing that you want to change—this thing that has you in a grip—is just too powerful and that you have to give up? Please, don't give up yet. You may just be on the verge of victory.

So often when people move through the change process, they quit just short of reaching their goal. Just when they've almost reached the pinnacle of their journey, they give up on the weight loss, new job opportunities, or relationships that could bring them happiness. Don't let this happen to you. When you feel that you might be close to quitting, double your efforts. Rally your supports. Reaffirm where you're going.

This feeling of wanting to quit can easily happen when you've hit a plateau, when people are questioning the wisdom of your choices, when you're not getting the results you expected, or when other things in your life have captured your attention.

Making personal change is not for the weak hearted. You're going to need all the resources and the determination you can muster to accomplish this challenging task. In the planning stages, spend some time anticipating other life events that may creep in to sidetrack you. As I was writing this book, my second grandchild was born. What a great sidetrack that was! It was an entirely delightful experience, but one that tempted me to put away my writing and focus entirely on the new baby.

Imagine breaking out of an old pattern that has trapped you for years. Imagine moving from a place of confusion to a place of clarity, commitment and finally, victory! Imagine the story that you will be able to tell about your own journey of change. Imagine the pride that you'll feel in telling everyone how you made the shift. How will you tell your story? Who will want to hear it? Who will notice how different you are without ever mentioning it. Just imagine!

Temptation Islands

"When choosing between two evils, I always like to try the one I've never tried before."
~ Mae West

BEING TEMPTED TO quit, give up or let go of your dream isn't the problem; but giving into that temptation is. Every ardent changer has been tempted at some point to skip the workout, ignore advice from a change buddy, omit due diligence, succumb to what everyone else is doing, have just one drink or behave in the old way one more time—just for old time sake. Being tempted is normal—it's how you handle the temptation that makes or breaks your movement forward. What could tempt you?

Have you ever watched Temptation Island? It's a television reality series which takes place in an exotic, warm locale, featuring young, attractive couples, who, after their arrival, are separated into male and female *camps* accompanied by stunningly gorgeous members of the opposite sex. Over a period of several weeks, participants have to choose whether they'll remain faithful to their original partner or succumb to 'temptation'. At the beginning of the show, each couple vows to remain committed to each other, but by the end of the show, few couples go home together.

Life can throw you a curve at any time. You may suffer injury in an accident, fall ill, lose your job, or be subjected to any number of things that can interrupt your plans for change. If major life events come along in the middle of your program, it may be necessary, and even wise, to put some things on hold temporarily. But don't make hasty decisions to postpone your change effort just because something else is vying for your attention. Make sure the circumstance warrants an interruption.

The temptation to quit is normal. Temptation is everywhere, and it's more dangerous when it takes you by surprise. Planning for temptation kicks it in the butt!

When you are faced with temptation to quit—be patient. Remember, things aren't always as they seem. Be willing to wait for success – the ability to persevere is what separates whiners from winners. Get great at the wait!

When you are being tempted is a great time to revisit your original Pleasure list. Remember, your reasons for making this change should be front and center at all times. Your goals should be plastered all over your house, in your day-timer and on your lips.

Avoid Revenge

"If you plan on revenge, better dig two graves."
~ *Chinese proverb*

ONE OF THE MOST common missteps people make when they're faced with unsolicited change, such as losing a job, being left by a partner, or being impacted by someone else's blunders, is to focus their energy on taking revenge. While it's natural to feel angry, frustrated, disappointed, abandoned or bewildered, it's not helpful to use your precious energy to seek revenge. Revenge requires negative energy and may put at risk your personal or professional reputation and your chances for successfully overcoming a tough situation.

Consider instead, taking the high road. Visualize how you really want to *be* in this situation. If you manage a difficult life or work challenge with dignity, grace and class, you will distinguish yourself as someone who is capable of managing stress, disappointment and challenge well, a skill-set that is in high demand in today's companies and families.

I recently worked with the VP of Human Resources of a large manufacturing company that was bought out by a foreign conglomerate. The VP was under tremendous pressure to serve a company filled with outraged employees, deal with relentless media and integrate hostile staff with the incoming leadership team all the while knowing it was unlikely his position would survive the merger. I watched as this astute change agent focused on the people and projects at hand, one grueling day at a time. He maintained a positive outlook, never denigrated the merging power structure and maintained his dignity and composure. Many times he had the opportunity to leak information and undermine the senior leadership's credibility, but he never did. When the merger was complete and he was let go, he secured a very senior position with a progressive company that was looking for someone with his well defined qualities—someone who had aptly demonstrated grace under fire.

When you're tempted to take revenge—don't.

Measuring Your Success

"Are we there yet?"
~ The annoying chant of every human
under the age of 12 on every road trip
they ever took with their parents.

MY COUNSELING CLIENTS have often asked me, "Am I getting better?" There were times when I was shocked by that question, as I could see significant ways in which they were improving; positive feedback from family and friends and a decreased need for medications were often the evidences to me that they were making progress. I often wondered how they could be so unaware of the positive changes that were obvious to those around them.

After many attempts at trying to reassure my clients that they were making progress, I learned to ask new clients to design a set of outcome measures *before* we began our work together. I explained that they would never know if they were *there* yet, if they didn't know where *there* was.

Whether you call them outcome measures or success metrics, it's always smart to chart your progress.

Mandy wanted to eliminate the tension that she always felt from her husband's family every time they got together. She spoke about the snide remarks her in-laws made about her parenting skills and the disparaging glances she received when she prepared meals for the extended family gatherings. She knew she was undeserving of this kind of criticism and it was affecting her relationship with her husband.

Here's the process Mandy and I designed to define specific measures for her change program.

1. I asked Mandy to define the current situation.
   She identified:

   - too much negative contact with her in-laws
   - feeling uncomfortable and unsafe in their home
   - responding passively when they made negative comments towards her.

2. Then I asked her to define what she wanted.
   She said:

   - decrease the number of visits with the offending family members
   - have most of the visits in her home, where she felt more comfortable
   - respond assertively when negative comments were made

3. And finally we quantified what she wanted.
   She decided to:

   - decrease her visits each year from 10 to 4
   - have three out of the four gatherings at her home
   - set boundaries with the in-laws and respond to criticism assertively

4. Then came the *by when* part of the process. Mandy established the following steps to ensure she would be successful with her goals.

   - Before Labor Day—within a six-month time frame she wanted to communicate her decision to the family members involved, including which functions and the locations she was prepared to attend.

   - By Christmas—within a nine-month time frame she wanted to learn to respond differently to her in-laws

At the end of the first month, Mandy had spoken with two of the families involved and she had met with me four times to build a repertoire of responses. That's progress! She continued to move forward with her goal each month, and by the end of the nine-month period, she had told all four families about her plan and had become very capable of responding assertively whenever they tried to intimidate her with their jibes.

Mandy had necessary milestones by which she could measure her progress. For example, during month four, while at a particularly difficult social gathering, she once again encountered her mother-in-law's wrath. She was shaken, but was able to keep her cool and chose to respond appropriately.

By having specific outcome measures she was able to remind herself that she only needed to get through two more family visits, and that despite the struggle, she had already accomplished significant stages of her goal.

Different change efforts call for different measures. Decide how you can track your progress. Be specific and record your plan. Tie the measures back to your original goals. Refer to them often, especially if you are becoming discouraged and feeling like you aren't making progress. Use charts, tape measures, scales, bank balances, course credits, or timelines—whatever will help you keep track of your particular progress.

Getting Serious About You

"Whenever he thought about it, he felt terrible.
And so, at last, he came to a fateful decision.
He decided not to think about it."
~ Life 101

CHANGE TAKES ENERGY and intense change calls for extreme self-care measures. What do I mean by extreme self-care? Think about going out on a beautiful winter day and gracefully gliding down the slopes at the local ski hill. Now picture yourself being set atop a 10,000 foot mountain range by helicopter, snapping on your skis and soaring to the bottom. That's the difference between your regular routine of self-care and the kind of care necessary for life in the change lane. To practice *extreme* self-care means to value yourself more than you ever have.

Extreme self-care means:

- increasing your normal fitness routine by half,

- fueling your body with nutritious, quality food choices,

- allowing 20 minutes each day to practice **SOS:** *Stop/ Observe What Is /Be Silent,*

- monitoring your self talk for negativity, and replacing self defeating chatter with positive self-affirming truths,

- monitoring what you read, hear, watch or participate in to see if it adds value to your life and ridding yourself of all the things that don't add value,

- limiting or eliminating time spent in negative relationships or with unsupportive people, and

- reconnecting to, or strengthening your spiritual roots.

It's important to consider yourself first during a personal transition. It's not selfish to care for yourself, it's smart. You can't help anyone else unless and until you have taken care of yourself.

Practicing extreme self-care invites you to notice what you really need, and encourages you not to always depend on others to fill those needs. Taking care of yourself means that you're capable of taking charge of your own life-nurturing so that you can offer your best to others.

Have Fun and Feel Good Too!

"I love to shop after a bad relationship. I don't know why. I buy a new outfit and it makes me feel better. It just does. Sometimes if I see a really great outfit, I'll break up with someone on purpose."
~ Rita Rudner

IN ANY SIGNIFICANT transition there will be some tough times to overcome. To scale the steep mountains of renewal you'll need to have a pack full of activites that make you feel good along the way. You'll need ways to recoup, regroup and rest for a while. And you'll need places and people with whom to laugh, play and just let go.

Feel-good activities don't always have to cost a lot or require the involvement of others. So, what's your pleasure? What inspires you? Where are your sources of encouragement? Where is your soft place to fall?

Here are some of mine:

- art that invites me to see the world a different way
- music that makes me want to dance
- poems that enrich my soul
- sleeping in
- bubble baths with candles
- playing with my grandchildren
- massages

- chocolate eaten slowly and guiltlessly
- long soulful walks among pine trees
- a good book that I've been waiting to read
- spicy Mexican food
- an amateur play
- long telephone conversations with my sister
- looking through old picture albums
- cleaning closets
- Dr. Pepper on ice!

So what's your pleasure? Be sure to schedule times of pure enjoyment on the way to your goals. It will make getting there much more fun!

Keep the Faith

"The real power behind whatever success I have now was something I found within myself—something that's in all of us, I think—a little piece of God just waiting to be discovered."
~ *Tina Turner*

PEOPLE OF FAITH make better changers. Sound like a bold statement? It is, and I absolutely believe it to be true. The founders of Alcoholics Anonymous knew that having faith in something greater than oneself was the underpinning of success. Hence, they have used the Serenity Prayer as their creed for several decades.

I've worked with thousands of people going through change and it has been my observation time and again that people who have strong spiritual ties are more resilient than those who don't have a spiritual connection or belief. We need all the help that we can get when we're making significant change, and having an active faith equips a serious changer in several ways.

The following poem showed up in my local newspaper on a day in my life when I really needed some guidance. I never found out who wrote it, but the words are powerful and I'd like to share them with you.

Do you need Me?
I am here!
You cannot see Me, yet, I am the light you see by.
You cannot hear Me, yet I speak through your voice.
You cannot hear Me, yet, I am the power at work through your hands.
I am at work, though you do not understand My ways.
I am at work, though you do not recognize My work.
I am not a strange vision.
I am no mystery.
I am here.
I hear.
I answer.
When you need Me, I am here.
Even if you deny Me, I am here.
Even in your doubts, I am here.
Even in your pain, I am here.
I am there when you pray and when you do not pray.
I am in you and you are in Me
Empty your heart of empty fears.
In yourself, you can do nothing, but I can do all.
I am in all.
Though you may not see the good, there is good and I am there.
Only in Me does the world have meaning.
Only in Me does the world take form.
I hung the stars and placed the planets in order.
I am the Love that is fulfilling.
I am the Assurance.
I am the Peace.
I am the Truth.
I am the Law that you can live by.
I am the Merciful One that you can cling to.
I am the One that will never leave you.
I am the One who will never turn His back on you.
I am.
Though you fail Me, I do not fail you.
Though your faith in Me is unsure, My faith in you never waivers!
I know you, I love you and I believe in you.
Beloved, I am here.

I believe that:

- Faith helps create a hopeful perspective. Trusting that there's divine help available, when you think you just can't go on, can instill courage and confidence in the face of difficult circumstances.

- A community of believers can be a vital support when you're choosing to grow and change. At the very heart of most faith based groups is the intention to promote personal and spiritual growth among its members. Having a group of people who support and understand your desire to grow and change can greatly add to your chances of success.

- Prayer works! Science has now proven that prayer lowers blood pressure and promotes healing. Being prayed for, whether you even know it's happening or not, makes you heal faster and more completely.

- Being connected to God connects you to others. You're part of a larger whole. When you get better, learn, achieve or advance, so do others.

- Most faith traditions have sacred writings that reveal eternal truths. Reading wisdom literature, like the Bible, gives you access to timeless truths and insight into life, yourself and the world around you. Change is unsettling. Having an anchor tied to ancient wisdom that can instruct, calm and inspire is priceless.

What are your spiritual beliefs? Perhaps you were raised in a faith tradition, but have let it go over the years, or maybe you've never known what it means to seek spiritual guidance. I strongly urge you to let today be the beginning of spiritual learning and reconnection for you as you travel on your journey.

171

Celebrating Your Success

"Victory goes to the player who
makes the next-to-last mistake."
~ Chess master Savielly Grigorievitch Tartakower

HOW WILL YOU celebrate when your *big fat change* is complete? Yes, I said celebrate! You've worked hard and you need to reward yourself for your bravery, effort, perseverance and success. Marking the small victories as you go along will help you stay energized and ready for the larger challenges still ahead.

A friend of mine was determined to finish university—no matter what. For three years, she sacrificed spending time with her family, buying new clothes, taking vacations, pursuing leisure activities and having fun while she immersed herself in attending classes, writing papers and chasing grades.

Each time she completed a semester, she'd rush on to the next set of classes without as much as a weekend off to reflect on her progress or enjoy the accomplishment. Big mistake. Eventually she quit just two semesters short of her degree because she had become physically and emotionally exhausted. When asked about her university experience, she was hard pressed to recall a single happy memory. She often refers to her time in university as, "the black period in my life." What a waste.

Stake out the territory of your transition. Identify the landmarks that will signal achievement along the way. Depending on your particular goal, decide how many resumes you need to send, phone calls you need to make, fights you need to avoid, quiet weekends you must navigate, embarrassing moments you want to avoid, pounds you want to lose, tears you need to cry, or how much money you need to save before you decide to take a break and celebrate. You don't have to be completely *finished* to enjoy the sweet taste of small victories.

Break your time into chunks. Whenever you pass through one stage, stop for a few hours, days or weeks—depending on the situation—and take some time to celebrate or rest.

Creating Your Success Story

Success stories are the feel-good anecdotes of life. How will you write yours? Here's an example:

Paula was an attractive young woman who had grown up with a mother that dragged her and her siblings from one unsuccessful marriage to another. By the time Paula was 15, she had lived with four different 'fathers' and 23 various stepbrothers and sisters. Each time her mother brought a new man into her children's lives, there were promises of a real family, a nice house and happiness. Each time Paula moved, she hoped that this would be the last, but without fail, each time she was disappointed. She suffered through the same routine over and over again.

At first, her mother would sing the praises of the new man; he was so sweet, so smart, and most importantly— 'not like the last jerk'. The family would enjoy a few months of family dinners, outings and attempts at blending all the children's lifestyles and personalities. But it always ended the same way. Paula's mother would slowly begin to find fault with the new man. He went from being a prince to a jerk in the blink of an eye. Each time, Paula would pull away and try to survive the fireworks that always came next. Eventually, she learned not to get involved with the new man and his kids. She withdrew into herself and decided that she couldn't trust men because they always changed.

As Paula grew into adulthood, she went through several disappointing relationships. They always started out well, but never lasted. She questioned why she always ended up with 'losers'. She was in the unconscious stage. She really didn't understand how her own behavior created her revolving-door relationship style.

Paula needed to experience something different in order to make better choices. Some of the change tools she chose to use in her program included a time-out where she refrained from having any type of relationship for six months. In that time she committed to doing the difficult emotional work of therapy to get to the root of the sadness and sense of abandonment that she had experienced in her early childhood.

During the Initiation phase of her program, she decided to purposely cultivate non-romantic friendshps with two men whom she knew to be reputable. This activity would challenge her internal schema that prevented her from trusting men. Paula also decided to talk to her mother about the long line of 'dads' she'd brought in and out of her life. She wanted to find out as much as she could about these men—to evaluate from an adult perspective if indeed they were the 'losers' her mother had portrayed them to be.

Within a few months she had gained a new perspective on men in her past and the part that she played in the demise of her own relationships. The test of her newly acquired skill-set came several months later when she began a romantic relationship with a new man.

This time she was armed with a different perspective. She was able to see her role in the new relationship through the eyes of an adult. When problems surfaced and she found herself drifting back to the old, 'men are jerks' way of thinking, she caught her self-talk early and adopted a more balanced way of managing the troubling issue. She also used the new behaviors that she had used with her male friends and began to ask for what she wanted and make decisions about how she reacted and responded.

When she found herself drifting back into old patterns, she relied on a commitment she had made with her best friend. Her friend was to confront her when she spoke negatively about her new boyfriend. They had agreed that

Paula could only speak about what she knew for sure, and not speculate about her boyfriend's motives. Then, as per her commitment to herself, if she felt like she was losing perspective, she'd schedule a session with me to reaffirm her goal of honoring herself and being fair in her appraisal of her boyfriend and his behavior towards her.

Paula's life is a real success story. She developed a plan to improve the quality of her life and worked it. She learned about her personal style and worked with it. She utilized just about every change tool available—and won!

The need to celebrate success is as important as any step in the process. If you don't reward yourself adequately, you may revert back to ineffective behavior, negative habits and self-defeating ways of thinking.

Go
Review

WELL, HERE YOU are! Look at you. Aren't you proud? Congratulations! You made the *big fat* change and you're feeling more confident, more capable and proud of the *new* you. You've reached your goal. You really have something to celebrate! What's your success story? Everyone who decides to change, sticks with it and comes out the other side deserves to write one. After all, you made it! You made the *big, fat change* and changed your life. Most people move through life paying very little attention to examining and improving themselves, but not you. You've worked hard—good for you!

Remembering how you were successful in the first place is very important now. You may want to review this section regularly. Keep these powerful ideas in front of you as you come to the end of the process. Remember the valuable lessons you've learned. Review each section and make a check-list for yourself.

- Do you recognize your dark alleys and danger zones? How are you avoiding them?

- When you're tempted, do you have methods and supports that can help you resist?

- Have you completely abandoned your notions of revenge?

- Do you have ways of measuring your success?

- How's your extreme self-care routine working?

- Are you having fun yet?

- Have you discovered new ways to *keep the faith* with yourself and God?

- How are you celebrating your success?

One Last Thing

Life can be cruel and changing can be tough. It can also
be hilarious! Some of the things you have done to work
your program, are just laughable. So, whatever else you do...
remember to laugh!

Laugh at yourself —laugh right out loud!

Chuckle at your own silliness
Be amused by the strength of your own stubbornness
Titter at your adversaries
Snicker at the height of your own stupidity
Hoot when you sense victory
Guffaw when you reach a milestone
Giggle with delight
when you recognize your own brilliance...again!

We have taken this journey together and I hope your trip was,
above all other things, *fun*. Becoming a healthier, happier,
more content, more focused, more successful *you* should be
fun...rip roaring fun!

Warmly,

Peggy

Bibliography:

Many wonderful authors have contributed to my learning. The men and women listed here represent some of the gifted writers who have influenced how I understand the process of change.

Adrienne, Carol. *The Purpose of Your Life*. New York: Eagle Book. 1998

Barker, Raymond Charles. *Treat Yourself to Life*. Marina Del Rey. De Vorss & Company Publishers. 1988

Beattie, Melody. *Beyond Codependency*. New York: Hazeldon Foundation. 1989

Beattie, Melody. *Codependent No More*. New York: Hazeldon Foundation. 1986

Bradshaw, John. *Family Secrets*. New York. Bantam Books. 1995

Chopra, Deepak. *Ageless Body Timeless Mind*. New York: Random House. 1998

Covey, Stephen R. *First Things First*. New York: Simon & Schuster. 1994

Day, Laura. *Practical Intuition*. New York. Broadway Books. 1996

Derman, Bruce, Ph.D. *We'd Have a Great Relationship if it Weren't for You*. Deerfield Beach. Health Communications. 1994

Goleman, Daniel. *Working With Emotional Intelligence*. New York: Banrum Books, 2000

Goleman, Daniel. *Emotional Intelligence*. New York: Banrum Books, 1995

Harris, Thomas, M.D. *I'm Ok – You're Ok*. New York: Harper & Row Publishers, Inc. 1969

Harvard Business School Press. *Crisis Management.* Harvard Business School Publishing. 1999

Harvard Business School Press. *Managing Uncertainty.* Harvard Business School Publishing. 1999

Harvard Business School Press. *Negotiation and Conflict Resolution.* Harvard Business School Publishing. 1999

Hendrix, Harville, Ph.D. *Getting the Love You Want.* New York: Harper & Row, Publishers. 1990

Hubble, Mark. Duncan, Barry. Miller, Scott. *The Heart and Soul of Change – What Works in Therapy.* Washington. American Psychological Association. 2002

Jeffers, Susan. *Feel the Fear and Do It Anyway.* New York: Ballantine Books. 1987

Johnson, Spencer, MD. *Who Moved My Cheese?* New York. G.P. Putnam and Sons. 1998

Kotter, John P. *Leading Change.* John P. Kotter. 1947

Perez, Edgardo & Wilkerson, Bill. *Mindsets.* Ottawa: The Homewood Centre for Organizational Health at Riverslea. 1998

Prochaska, James, et.all. *Changing for Good.* New York: Avon Books. 1995

Scott, Susan. *Fierce Conversations.* New York: Penguin Books Ltd. 2002

Seligman, Martin. *Learned Optimism.* New York: Simon & Schuster, Inc. 1990

Senge, Peter. *The Dance of Change.* New York: Doubleday.1999

Tannen, Deborah, Ph.D. *You Just Don't Understand.* New York: HarperCollins. 1989

Vanzant, Iyanla. *Yesterday I Cried*. New York: Simon &
Schuster. 1998

Viorst, Judith. *Necessary Losses*. New York: Ballantine
Books. 1986

Peggy Grall is in the business of helping individuals and groups realize their dreams.

In her early career as a Psychotherapist and now in her role as a Certified Coach, Trainer and Certified Speaking Professional, she has partnered with people from all walks of life, helping them to first decide what they want to achieve, and then to do it!

Her book "Just Change It!" reflects her wisdom in helping people to clarify what they want to change, choose the optimum time to begin and how to reach out and get the best support for their journey.

Other Books & Resources by Peggy Grall

Books/Workbooks:
- Just Change It! – Workbook
- The Change Style Index
- The One Thing: Change What You Thought You Couldn't

Booklets:
- 19 Hopeful Hints for Managing the Big Fat Changes at Work
- Change Bytes: Wit & Wisdom for Change Champions

Audio CD's:
- Working With Your Personality – Not Against It!
- Who are These People and Why are They Driving Me Crazy?
- Coaching Tips: Volume 1
- Leading Change & Learning to Love It!
- Now What Do I Say?: Making Friends With The Media

For more information on Peggy's products and programs please visit www.PeggyGrall.com or call 1.866.949.6698